fun with

Messy Play

of related interest

Small Steps Forward
Using Games and Activities to Help Your Pre-School Child with Special Needs
Second edition
Sarah Newman
Illustrated by Jeanie Mellersh
ISBN 978 1 84310 693 7

Playing, Laughing and Learning with Children on the Autism Spectrum
A Practical Resource of Play Ideas for Parents and Carers
Second Edition
Julia Moor
978 1 84310 608 1

Narrative Approaches in Play with Children
Ann Cattanach
ISBN 978 1 84310 588 6

Autism, Play and Social Interaction
Lone Gammeltoft and Marianne Sollok Nordenhof
Translated by Erik van Acker
ISBN 978 1 84310 520 6

fun with

Messy Play Ideas and
Activities for
Children
with Special
Needs

Tracey Beckerleg

Jessica Kingsley Publishers
London and Philadelphia

First published in 2009
by Jessica Kingsley Publishers
116 Pentonville Road
London N1 9JB, UK
and
400 Market Street, Suite 400
Philadelphia, PA 19106, USA
www.jkp.com

Library of Congress Cataloging in Publication Data
Beckerleg, Tracey.
 Fun with messy play : ideas and activities for children with special needs / Tracey Beckerleg.
  p. cm.
 ISBN 978-1-84310-641-8 (pb : alk. paper)
 1. Children with disabilities--Recreation. 2. Sensorimotor integration. 3. Motor learning. 4. Play therapy. 5. Creative activities and seatwork. I. Title.
 GV183.6.B43 2009
 790.1'96--dc22

                                                                2008017781

British Library Cataloguing in Publication Data
A CIP catalogue record for this book is available from the British Library

ISBN 978 1 84310 641 8

Printed and bound in Great Britain by
Athenaeum Press, Gateshead, Tyne and Wear

To my wonderful, long-suffering husband Will, who has
listened to my ideas with patience
for many years, and whose support and love
I value greatly, with much love.

Contents

Part One:
An Introduction to Messy Play

Part Two:
Benefits of Messy Play

Part Three:
Practical Messy Play Ideas

Preface

My name is Tracey Beckerleg and I am married to Will. We have five children and we live in Southampton. I have been working with children with additional support needs since I was 13, when my dad's friend introduced me to his eight-year-old son Alan who had cerebral palsy. Soon afterwards I went along to the school he attended – the White Lodge Centre in Chertsey in Surrey – and, as you could in those days, began to go into the school to help. In the holidays the school used to run a holiday club; I went along to help with that and did so until I went to college in 1982.

I trained at Matlock College of Higher Education in Derbyshire to be a teacher of children with severe learning difficulties. There I was able to start exploring messy play and used it in some of my teaching practices. I taught full-time for five years once qualified and found that in my work with children with more complex needs, messy play just kept on being successful and I became more and more interested in it.

I then went on to have my five children, all of whom have taken a full part in messy play at home – I suppose you could say that they were my 'guinea-pigs'. There is nothing that I haven't done with them, in fact their dad used to wonder what he was going to find when he came home from work. If you ask my children, they will say that the things that they remember most are the fun we had with mess.

Since returning to work I have worked as a pre-school play practitioner. For the past four years I have been employed as a Portage

Home Visitor, working with children with additional support needs and their families in the home and more recently running a small lunchtime group with children with delays in social, communication and behavioural skills.

I think my colleagues were more than a little surprised by my activities, and I have quickly become renowned among the families. Often the first words that greet me on arrival at a new family are: 'Oh, you're the messy one!' I love messy play and in my work I use it all the time. I have seen again and again that it is a valuable tool. It does get great results and it is such fun!

I decided to write this book after much nagging from my husband. He has listened to my ideas for years and has continually told me that I should get them down on paper.

Thus began a year of trying to put all my thoughts into some sort of order, and to see if I could find some other research on the subject. I used the computer to search for any articles on messy play and discovered that you have to be careful what you key into a search engine. There were some very strange articles that appeared in relation to my searching, certainly with no relation at all to my book title.

Writing this book has been like running a marathon. I was progressing well and then I hit the 17,000 word mark and found that I had a mental block and it was so hard to overcome. I just wanted to give up. However, some good friends and colleagues really began to encourage me when I reached that point, and a bit like the 18-mile marathon 'wall', I suddenly gained more energy and enthusiasm and whizzed past.

Throughout this book I have referred to the child as either *him* or *her*. I have used the terms *special educational needs* and *additional support needs* to refer to the needs of the children I am aiming this book at, because it would appear that at present these terms are interchangeable. When I have named a product by brand, this is not to endorse one brand name over another; I am simply relaying by own experience. By typing any of those brands into an internet search engine, you can discover a whole range of similar products before making a purchase.

I am hoping that this book will appeal to all those involved with children with additional needs. It's not a book solely for professionals – I trust that it is an easily understandable and usable book. It has some technical stuff in it, but that's just there to help the readers understand why they will do what they do.

This was emphasised to me by a family I was once working with. We had spent half an hour playing with tangerine jelly. It was a very hot day and what had started out as a cold wobbly lump quickly became a slushy and sticky liquid! We had all had great fun poking, pushing and squeezing the jelly but as it liquefied we began to splash and managed to cover ourselves, the room and the child in very sloppy jelly. Smiling hugely and covered in tangerine jelly, his white shirt speckled with orange, the dad turned to me and said: 'That was fun, so why exactly are we doing this?'

It has been immensely satisfying finally to commit my ideas to paper, and I hope that they prove useful. I hope that smiles, fun and laughter are experienced as activities are attempted. But don't be afraid, it's just mess and will always wash up.

Just one thing to remember – these are purely my ideas and activities that I have found have accomplished great steps with the children with whom I have had the privilege to work, for 20 years. It is not an answer to all problems and will not suddenly help to perform great miracles. However, I do believe that these ideas will help to produce little stepping stones along the way to greater goals. And best of all, it's all great fun!

So go ahead – GET MESSY!

Tracey Beckerleg

Acknowledgements

To my husband Will and my children Ruth, Josh, Sarah, Jess and Kerenza, who have had to put up with all my ideas and experiments over the years. Especially Will, who has had to listen to all my adventures and has helped me to put things properly when I got tangled up in my thoughts, and who checked all my spelling, grammar and punctuation and untied all the confusions.

To all my friends at Southampton Portage who have encouraged me to produce this book – especially Maggie, who first suggested I approach Jessica Kingsley Publishers.

To Zillah and Mel, who proofread my book and gave me great encouragement.

To Judy Denziloe for allowing me to adapt her laminate pocket ideas, which she first used in sensory books, into the messy play pockets that I use today.

To all the members of the UK Semiochemistry Network – a small group of scientists, chemists and ordinary members of the public who are interested in the sense of smell. I went to a conference that they held in July 2007 where I learnt a considerable amount of information about the sense of smell and how it operates. It was this information that helped me to understand the sense of smell in regard to the children with whom I work. If you ever want to know anything about smell, they are the people to contact.

To all my families who helped with the photos and were happy for me to include their children in the book – Debbie, Charlie and

Frankie Witt; Dionne, Jez and Cariad Howat; and Toni, Andrew and Ben Goodchild.

Finally, to all the ladies who attended the workshops at the Portage conference in Northampton in 2007 and who insisted I finish my book.

To all these people who helped me along the way… Thank you.

Part One

AN INTRODUCTION TO MESSY PLAY

1 WHY DO MESSY PLAY?

When I meet any of my families for the first time, I am frequently greeted with: 'Oh, you're the messy one!' My fame goes before me! Now that phrase can be taken one of two ways: they are either really excited about the prospect or they are absolutely dreading it.

I can well imagine that as you are reading this you are experiencing one of these two feelings too. You are probably wondering why on earth anyone would want even to contemplate playing with mess or messy things, or you may be really curious to know what it is all about. I hope that I will be able to satisfy both questions during the course of this book.

How I CAME TO DISCOVER MESSY PLAY

I don't think I discovered it, more it discovered me. I have always been messy. From an early age I was in the garden cooking with weeds and earth; filling the sandpit with water; digging a muddy hole to discover water or Australia, whichever came first; making perfume from stagnating rose petals; and making ice-cream from milk and butter and leaving it by the fire to set! As a child, there's no doubt – I enjoyed being messy. I have continued this theme into my adult life and have enjoyed a great deal of messy play with my own children. They all have great memories of hands on and in cooking from as soon as they could sit up in a highchair, as well as painting their whole bodies and making body prints. If I can do it with five children so can you.

I think it's the word 'messy' that sends chills down the most reasonable person's spine. You probably have visions of custard-pie flinging activities, such as is sometimes seen on children's television programmes, or of small children eating chocolate and then smearing chocolatey fingers on the walls or furniture. However, there is nothing messy that I use that cannot be cleaned up and sorted out quickly with some soap and water. So settle down, relax and prepare to be amazed.

THE ORIGINAL IDEA OF MESSY PLAY

Messy play has been around for years. People – yes, even grown-ups – have been engaging in messy play for many years, but most people do not call it this. There have always been programmes on the television that have encouraged adults to take part in team games that call for a considerable amount of mess. The teams are prepared to put themselves into activities and situations that they would not dream of doing in their normal everyday lives. The games might call for contestants to dress up, wear large boots, climb onto a pair of stilts, walk across a wobbly bridge carrying buckets of some disgusting substance ('gunge'), and if the substance hasn't dropped on them or they haven't fallen over, it is poured into a measuring tube at the end of the course and the team with the most in the tube wins the game. These programmes have appeared on television screens all over the world. They have varying names but include similar activities, with presenters roaring with laughter at the contestants' antics. Although some of the programmes have received a lot of complaints, they continue to draw huge audience figures because people like to see other people getting messy. The formula is very successful, and the ethos behind them has continued to influence other programmes. Gunge is regularly seen on the small screen now.

This is actually messy play, but because it mainly involves adults and it happens on the television, most people just call it entertainment and are very glad that they do not have to be actually involved.

Very young children engage in messy play automatically, beginning when they 'play' with their food during finger feeding, but unfortunately this activity is often frowned upon and the child is told he is 'dirty' and he soon stops.

Children love to explore and will naturally be drawn to all that is messy – e.g. mud, earth, water, paint, glue. However, this is not always encouraged as we, their parents, guide them quickly towards other activities that are more acceptable. We live in a clean society, obsessively clean sometimes. Just think of all the adverts on the television. Germs have no place in our society; they have to be killed 'dead'. We all have to have exceptionally clean houses, after all that is what everyone who is anyone has. Clean is the new fashion accessory. In this growing climate of cleanliness it is no surprise that messy play is considered unacceptable. Houses, schools, public buildings have to be kept clean and no one wants them to be messed up.

In schools and pre-schools when one considers messy play, the usual things that come into mind are sand, paint, glue and water. These are and always have been wonderful media to use, but they are not very exciting in a sensory way.

That is why I decided to look at messy play in a new way and explore new means of engaging with children and families.

MESSY PLAY AND ME

Before I was a mum I was a full-time teacher of children with severe learning difficulties. It was in this job that I fully discovered the joys of messy play and how beneficial it can be. At first, messy play was confined to lots of paint, water, shredded paper and polystyrene chips. We had lots of fun and the children enjoyed their experiences, but I felt there was something more I could do.

In 1987 I was asked to develop a special science curriculum for my class of 16 children who all experienced profound and multiple learning difficulties. At that time there were no P levels and no established curriculum to be followed since the National Curriculum was only just being introduced. However, I felt that these children should be included in the new national curriculum framework in some way and set about devising a science curriculum that would be appropriate for them and tailored to their individual needs.

I thought about the children and their needs and decided that they needed a lot of experiences to be brought to them because many of them found it very difficult to involve themselves. I wanted it to be exciting, motivating and different, and above all I wanted it to be fun. I had wonderful classroom assistants who were willing to try anything, and they became used to my new ideas and the sudden changes in the classroom. Whatever we were doing, the classroom 'became' the subject.

So, if we explored water, the classroom became an underwater scene with crepe seaweed and fish hanging from the ceiling. When we were learning about rain and it didn't rain for weeks, we all went outside dressed in wellies, placed bowls of water on the ground for splashing in and a helper poked a hose out of the window, turned it on and hosed the huge fishing umbrellas we held. What a wonderful sound and what fun!

From here we moved on to food and explored everything to do with its smell, texture, taste and colour. Our favourite activity was exploring thick banana milkshake and making smelly, textured pictures.

We also explored mini-beasts and dipped them in paint to watch how they moved across a perspex sheet. The children experienced them moving on their hands, felt their coolness and with some of them their wetness. It was very messy and caused great laughter, good eye contact and some very fine, careful movements. Of course, it was all easily and readily cleaned up.

I have to place a note of caution here and say that I would not recommend playing with mini-beasts any more. I was a young and enthusiastic teacher and I would have tried anything to gain eye contact – I have even been known to dye my hair bright pink just to get a child to look at me (and by the way it did work!). It is just an example of how I was prompted to explore the subject of messy play. As the years have gone by, many health and safety protocols have been put in place which would now prevent this activity being carried out. Also I imagine that many people would feel that placing creatures in paint was not a very kind thing to do.

Another experience was that of cooking. For my class it was a whole messy play session. It involved turn taking, because we only used one big bowl and passed it around. The children developed their own observational skills watching the activities of the other children and the ingredients in the bowl. They learnt to accept working in a group and having someone else next to them. They touched each ingredient and explored the cooking at each stage of its creation. They also enjoyed heightened smell stimulation as they stayed in the kitchen whilst their creation was cooking. At the end, each child enjoyed some watery, bubbly messy play as the washing-up was carried out. It was tremendous fun.

Once I became a mum I drew on these experiences when playing with my children, and messy play became very much a part of our daily experience as a family. My poor husband never quite knew what he was going to come home to, but my children, now aged 10 to 18, have some wonderful memories, especially of crawling through a giant pretend ear in the garden to understand the journey of sound through the ear to the brain and splashing in water-filled sandpits in bare feet in the middle of February – at their request of course!

So WHY DO MESSY PLAY?

Well, first I think I should include a couple of quotes – after all what is a book without some quotes? The first one is this...

I have direct contact with the medium which helps me to understand perception and increases my awareness of texture. It is soothing and I have no expectations placed on me for a finished product. (Southbridge School, New Zealand)

This is one of the best quotes about messy play. It emphasizes the relaxing side of it and the fact that through it a child's sensory perceptions can be heightened. It is also an ideal way of helping a child begin to understand and interact with the world around him. It also places no demands on the child, there is no expected way for him to react. It is all about the child, the media and his response to it, which can then be built upon.

The second quote, from *Wonderplay* (1995) br Fretta Reitzes and Beth Teitelman, is this…

Children learn through active use of all their senses.

Messy play is active and it makes good use of all senses, it is not a passive activity.

Now back to the question 'Why do messy play?' Well, I do it because…

Messy play is fun!

I use messy play in my work for the reasons given in the above quotes and for many other reasons, but the main one is that it is FUN! You may be doubtful and worried about the mess, but the fact that it is so much fun makes up for that. I know as you are reading this you probably don't believe me, but it really is. If you do just a little bit of messy play each day (start small so that it is easy to tidy up), you soon lose all worries about sticky hands and funny smells. As you see the children relaxing, responding and having fun, you too will begin to believe that this is fun.

Messy play is different

Well, if you engage in messy play you will certainly be doing something different. It will be like nothing you have done before. It is not like paint and water, although I do still use these in messy play. It smells, has some wonderful textures, looks unusual and has many varying forms, and because of this…

It can produce amazing results that wouldn't necessarily be seen elsewhere

I know this is a big claim to make, but I have seen children's motor skills, language skills and cognitive skills all improved through consistent, regular sessions with messy play. These are some specific areas of improvement I have observed:

- relaxation of muscles
- development of gross and fine motor skills
- development of self-help skills
- development of social play, turn taking and sharing
- development of concentration and observation skills
- development of bonding
- development of body awareness
- development of communication skills.

I will explore these claims later in the book, but here I would like to give an example of a child's improvement after some messy play sessions.

When I first began working with messy play in the home, I was working with a child who was unable to communicate about his needs. He used photographs to indicate what he wanted but it was always in an uncontrolled grabbing way – so much so that the photos quickly became crumpled and unusable. His parents wanted him to be able to indicate by pointing. We used Angel Delight and then jelly, at first using large hand movements to squeeze and explore, then moving on to using one finger to poke it in a small container. We continued with paint placed in film pots so that he had to use only one finger to access the paint, and eventually we went on to Hula Hoops placed on the photo. Once we had achieved pointing through the

Hula Hoops, we began to move them gradually away from the photo, until one week he pointed without a Hula Hoop and began to point without using them at all. Eventually he transferred this learning to the world around him, and our goal was achieved.

This is one simple example of success with messy play, and I will give many more as the book progresses. For now, I hope I have stimulated your interest enough to want to continue to read and discover more.

2 PLAY AND ITS PURPOSE

How many times have you heard this conversation or seen this scenario?

A small boy is happily exploring a muddy puddle with a stick and along comes Mum. 'Oh Ben, stop that!' she says. 'You'll get messy!'

Or perhaps this little scene:

A small girl is playing happily on the floor with a saucepan and a wooden spoon banging the saucepan with the spoon, making lots of noise and having a great time. Along comes Mum. 'Gemma, for goodness sake, why are you making that noise?'

Here we have two children who are enjoying that thing that we as adults so often seem to have forgotten how to do. They are playing! While they are playing they are learning. So many people today just do not recognize the value of play.

In our culture, as adults we are generally obsessed with targets and goals, and increasingly we are transferring this onto our children. From the moment our child is born we compare our little one to our friend's baby or his older siblings. We want to know whether the baby has smiled, sat, said the first word, slept through the night, been potty trained or walked. We compare him endlessly to charts in baby books, we look at Dr Spock and Penelope Leach and wonder and sometimes fret whether our baby is doing what he should for his age.

I have to say that I was also like this with my first child, but moderated somewhat with second and subsequent children. After our second child was born (and third as well because we had twins!) I discovered that, as my sister-in-law Sally says, 'second babies bounce better'. By this she means that as parents we are all more organized, a bit less stressy and a bit more laid back with our second and subsequent babies than we were with our first. Once we have experienced our first baby, we know what a baby does and what to expect, and because of this experience we are not so worried or uptight about everything.

When our first child, Ruth, was born, I was my own worst enemy. Having been to college and carried out a study on children in long-stay hospitals and the effect that lack of attention and nurturing can have on a child, you could say that I was obsessed with giving my little one as much attention as possible. I worried about her not being entertained constantly, so I never left her alone. Even when she was in her pram or playpen she was surrounded by activities that would move or make a sound if she touched them.

As well as these things, what my little girl needed was time to herself, time to explore by herself, time to discover about her environment at her own pace, a little bit of *me* time. However, what she got was adult-directed activity, adult-initiated activity and constant adult attention. All that she learnt was directed by myself and was what I wanted her to learn. I now realize that that was not a good way to help a little person learn. Sure, she has benefited from this in that she is incredibly bright and performs well at school, she satisfies all the school's league tables, but I'm not so sure that she hasn't missed something along the way.

Children are all different, and we cannot and should not treat them as pieces of meat passing through a mincer that are all exactly the same and emerge as the same sausages at the end (to use the imagery employed in Pink Floyd's *The Wall* video). Children are not an experiment to see how many grades they can achieve, either for their parents or schools or the government of the day. What so many educationalists forget is that children are individuals. They are all different and should sometimes be allowed to explore their own strengths and weaknesses at their own pace.

In this respect there is so much that children can learn through the medium of play – sometimes directed and sometimes most definitely undirected – and that is why it is so important that children are offered, allowed and actively given the opportunity to play.

Everyone, if they would only admit it, enjoys play. We begin to learn this skill as a child, and it continues with us right through to adulthood, although as adults, we often do not call it play.

Many of us have enjoyed a 'Murder Mystery Party' or an '80s Night Out'. Part of the fun at these events is that we can dress up and pretend to be someone else. Some of us help out at Guides, Scouts, ATC and other uniformed organizations because then we can join in the activities and play. Of course we don't say that, it's helping the children really. How many of us really enjoy the adult theme parks and adventure areas because we can be 'big kids' as we enjoy all the rides? Perhaps we secretly enjoy Punch and Judy or pantomimes when we go with our children because we can be a child again and shout at the baddies, cheer the goodies and tell the bad guy that 'It's behind you!' We all love play, even as adults. It is a chance to hang up our cares for a little while and just enjoy a tremendous sense of freedom.

So why is play so important for children? It is a means by which they can learn and explore the world around them safely. It is a means of helping all sorts of skills develop. What better way to help gross motor skills develop than by playing in the garden, learning to climb, kicking a ball, playing games with siblings and parents? Equally self-help skills are learnt when children dress up, play tea parties, dig in the sand and splash in the water, and cook in the kitchen with Mum. Many thinking or cognitive skills are learnt incidentally through our response to our environment. A toddler sitting on the floor in the kitchen learns, by experimenting with the saucepans and wooden spoons, that pots and pans can be banged and that they are noisy. Through exposure to repetitive stories they learn that there is a rhythm and routine to everyday life. It is through play that children test their ideas, ask questions and come up with answers. Language is also a skill that definitely improves and develops through play.

In so much of life there is a correct time and a place to carry out activities – for both children and adults. However, I believe that play should be also a place and time whereby the child is free to experiment, free to try out new skills that he might have learnt elsewhere, and indeed free to learn something new.

I also understand that with children with additional support needs it is often difficult for them to transfer a skill learnt in one place to another. This is why I believe that the play situation gives many opportunities to try out and consolidate any new skills learnt elsewhere. And messy play provides all of the opportunities that other sorts of play give.

TYPES OF PLAY

At this point I feel it is worth pointing out that with messy play as with all other sorts of play there are different types of play opportunities that can be offered. They include:

- making up rules
- experimental play
- non-directed play
- mirrored play
- structured directed play.

Making up rules

The play that I engaged in with my own daughter as described earlier was far from spontaneous. When she played, she played by my rules, I told her what to do, I set up the situation and often I chose the toys she played with. Looking back, I am sure that at times she was immensely frustrated by this. The arrival of her brother and sister meant that I had to divide my attention, which gave her some relief from my continual direction and the opportunity to explore by herself for the first time.

In messy play it is important to give time for the children to make up their own rules. Sometimes having to follow adult rules in a game can mean that a child constantly fails because he is having always to do what the adult says, at the time and pace dictated by the adult. This can lead to the child giving up or just not trying. When a child is allowed to explore and play in his own time and at his own pace, he may not follow all the rules set by adults but he will adapt them to what he can do, and this will become his rule until he can play using the set rules.

An example of this would be when I played Monopoly as a child. I could not understand the full game rules so my sister and I made up our own simplified rule system, which enabled us to play to the level we could cope with. The game manufacturers have caught on to this and have since brought out a children's version of their game, with a simpler board and simpler rule structure, which makes the game more accessible to a younger audience.

In letting the child play within the framework of his own rules he is having success at the level he can cope with and the success can then be built upon.

For example when playing with lentils I usually use a large cat litter tray and fill it with lentils. Then I give a child a scoop and with hand-over-hand help he will scoop the lentils and lift and place them into a small tub placed at the opposite end of the tray. We will do this several times and then I allow the child to play without my help. What often happens is that he will then spend a lot of time just scooping and letting the lentils fall, then he will move onto scooping them up with his hands and placing them in the tub. Then he will scoop them to the other side of the tray and eventually will scoop and place in the tub. Generally, he has to have all of these other experiences and learn, making his own set of rules, before he will follow mine and scoop across the tray and drop the lentils into the tub. I could make him follow my rules and continue with the hand-over-hand work, insisting that he does what I want, but this would probably result in a struggle over who holds the spoon, so that eventually the child either gives up or gives in and will perform the task without having learnt anything useful that can be transferred to other situations.

Experimental play

Messy play is great for this. So many of the toys that are available in our shops and stores are 'educational' and are there to teach something. If, for example, a child uses a bead abacus just to post the beads on and does not match colours or count, some people would feel the urge to direct the child to take on these additional activities. Perhaps you might hear an adult say 'That's not what that's for' or 'Let me show you how to do this' in an attempt to direct the child towards the more valuable activities that can be performed with an abacus. If the child is taught solely to focus on matching colours and counting on, he will learn these skills and concepts but will miss out on others. He will miss putting just one ball on a long pole and taking it off again. He will miss trying to put too many on one pole and then the excess ones falling off. He will miss making patterns with the colours. He will miss rolling the balls together and poking his finger through the hole in the ball to see what it feels like and if his finger will fit. There are many more potential activities which can be undertaken with an abacus than just the 'educational ones' of colour matching and counting on. These can be explored best as self-directed activities and have much to add to his experience and learning.

That is why messy play is so wonderful. There is no right or wrong way to do anything. Everything is new and exciting and there to be explored and discovered. It is through experimentation and exploration that children discover that tinned tomatoes have an infinite array of uses. They can just 'mess around' and have fun, because fun is at the heart of what messy play is all about.

Non-directed play

It is important not to feel that you as the adult always have to be in charge of the play. Deep down, we all like to be in charge because then we are in control – nothing takes us by surprise and nothing is going to happen that we cannot anticipate. However, this is not always necessary and certainly is not much fun! Sometimes we need to create times when there is the freedom to 'go with the flow', taking the moment and living in it – *carpe diem* or 'seize the day', as is said.

I know it is easier to be in control and to know, from my earlier example, that the spoon of lentils is going to be calmly and efficiently poured into the box. But wouldn't it be so much more fun if you just sat back and let your child explore the moment under his own steam, saying to yourself 'OK, let's see what happens.'

To relinquish control – even for a brief period – can be scary. You can end up with lentils all over the floor, you might be covered in jelly or squirty cream like I have done frequently, but just think what your child will have learnt. He will have learnt about colour, shape, texture, that jelly is slippery and cold and that cream smells strange, that if he slaps his hand down in the jelly it splats over him and the grown-ups around and that they then make a loud noise! It may not be easy to allow this to happen but it is worth it when you see the child's reactions. It is fun!

You could also try just commenting on what the child is doing. Describing his actions will help to explain his activity to him and will also encourage his language skills. Doing this does feel very strange for a little while and you can feel very silly doing it, but once you have started and have become comfortable it is very easy to just slip into it, almost forgetting that you are doing it. I would not say that you want to be doing this for too long, but probably ten minutes in any one session would be enough.

Mirrored play

This is like non-directed play in that you do not actually structure the child's play yourself or tell or show him what to do. This is where you copy what the child does.

For example if you are using a bowl of tinned tomatoes with the child, then you have a bowl as well as the child having his bowl. If the child splats his hand in them, then you do the same. If he makes a circular motion in them, then you do the same. This helps the child to become more engaged in play himself. He may be at the stage where he can tolerate someone sitting by him but otherwise ignores their activity. When he notices that someone is copying his activities, it may encourage his awareness and help to engage him in some play with the other person.

If you want to do this, it is probably best at first if you have your own bowl of tomatoes. Later you can play in the same bowl as the child and just use one bowl between you. I work with a child who will remove my hand from the bowl if I try to mirror activities in his bowl, but who is quite happy for me to mirror if I have my own bowl. Eventually I would hope to move on to engaging in play in his bowl.

Mirroring also gives the child a chance to be in control of play. He can see that what he does matters. He gets to lead and he gets to decide what happens. This will give some sense of satisfaction and positive reward, and these factors will influence a desired behaviour happening again.

Structured directed play

Structured directed play also has its place in messy play. Sometimes a child does have to be shown what to do because a new experience can be quite overwhelming, or indeed scary, and so he will be unsure how to react. In these circumstances some adult direction will help to overcome the child's natural apprehension at facing something for the first time. Adult direction will also be necessary if the aim of the session is to learn a specific skill.

Directed play can provide security and safety for a child who is unsure what is going to happen. It can provide a structure and a routine and a measure of predictability which together enable the child to be sure of his boundaries. It certainly has its place within the realm of messy play.

A good mixture

All of the above strategies can be used to good effect to create a lively and varied programme of messy play-based activities for the child. As in all activities, it is good to use a mixture of all these approaches when engaging in messy play. Variety is, as is said, the spice of life and using all of these approaches during a play session will maintain interest and help to develop the child's own play skills.

REMEMBER

Play is not just for children. The ability to play is a skill that we all need to cultivate and maintain. I do hope that during these messy play sessions you too will play and have as much fun as the children!

GUIDELINES FOR MESSY PLAY

In order to have a successful and productive messy play activity you need:

- an aim
- a plan
- the equipment you will use
- an evaluation.

WHAT ARE YOUR AIMS?

As with any activity you need to have a plan and a purpose when you carry out messy play. It is no good going in with no aim or preparation and expecting everything to go smoothly. Therefore you need to think:

What are your aims in doing this?

That's 'teacher speak' for Why are we doing this? Everyone has aims in life. We wake up in the morning and think, now what am I going to do today? Even if we don't actually write it down on paper, we have a plan in our head about how the day will progress. There are very few people who wake up and think I'll just take whatever the day throws at me! That is too scary!

It's exactly the same in messy play. We need to have an idea as to where we want to go, what do we want it to achieve, what are we going to use and how long are we going to continue.

It's no good just thinking 'Oh, I've got a tin of baked beans in the cupboard, I think I'll use those.' While spontaneity can have its place, this is not it, and this kind of thinking is likely to lead to an unsuccessful time, with you, the child and everyone else failing to enjoy it and everyone deciding that they never want to engage in this sort of play again.

PLANNING
People factors

Messy play is an exciting thing to embark upon. However, before you start there are a number of things you will need to think about in relation to her, their family and the particular experience you are offering them.

THE CHILD

It's important to remember that whilst messy play is a really exciting experience for you, it may not be felt that way by the child. Imagine this… you're two years old, you've just woken up and had breakfast, the door bell rings and in comes a very loud person dragging behind her a clattery trolley full of toys which keep making loud and unexpected noises. She sits down and after a chat with Mum, she puts in front of you a tray full of some wet, lumpy orange stuff. Then she takes hold of your hands and gently but firmly plunges them into it. It's cold, wet and sticky and you don't like it. You certainly don't want to touch it! You pull your hands away…she smiles and gently puts them back…you pull away again…she smiles again and puts your hands back in…you cry and think why does she want to do this, why doesn't she leave you alone…it's cold and it's scary…Mum picks you up. That's nice and it all stops.

What's wrong with this? Well there was no preparation to start with. Everyone needs to have time to get ready for new experiences. It would have been good to have Mum sitting close by or for the child to sit on Mum's lap, that would have calmed everyone. Perhaps the wet texture was not a good one to start with.

When introducing messy play you always need to put yourself in the child's position and consider how she may react to the experience you are giving her. How would I like this? What would I feel like? Is this something the child has not liked on a previous occasion and can the experience be changed or modified to make it more enjoyable? Mess purely for mess's sake or just because you think it would be a good idea is not the best reason to begin. It is always good to think carefully about the activity, to plan what you are going to do and how you are going to do it and know exactly what you expect to achieve through giving the child this particular experience.

Make sure you check for any allergies before you introduce any foodstuffs into the session. It would seem that today our children are more susceptible to allergies than ever before. For example, there are many more and younger cases of asthma, which can often be triggered by an allergic reaction. Therefore in all messy play it is best to avoid anything containing nuts, and that would include anything containing almond oil. Tomatoes can also cause rashes on the skin and this should be checked as well. Many children are milk and lactose intolerant, even soya can cause allergies.

It should also be remembered that there are many children who are gluten intolerant, and in these situations it is probably best to use rice flour. When using shaving foam or any cosmetic materials it would be best to use only those which are hypoallergenic or labelled as being suitable for sensitive skin types. And in these days of preservatives, flavourings and additives, be very careful when using highly coloured or flavoured materials.

Bear in mind also that highly coloured materials can stain clothing, skin and containers, and if the materials are being used very exuberantly and are flying around the room, they could stain furniture or walls. So make sure you ask that the child be dressed in old clothes, which won't matter when mess falls on them.

THE FAMILY

As grown-ups we do enjoy messy play, but we really enjoy the structured side of this. 'Oh yes,' I can hear you say, 'and what sort of messy play do you mean? I don't do mess in any shape or form!' Well, I don't mean messing with paint or food or anything like that. However, many of us enjoy massage with fragranced oils, or a sauna, or spa baths and hot tubs, or even mud packs. Even more of us really enjoy a day at the beach, which will almost always include playing in the sand. This is all messy play but in a very controlled and ordered way. These are familiar activities for most of us and well within our comfort zones.

However, when the words 'messy play' are first mentioned to families it can be a major shock. After all, how many people want mess in their homes? We all have our homes how we want them and the idea of someone wanting to introduce mess into it can be a little disconcerting to say the least.

Try to convince the family that they do not have to clean the home before you arrive. In one family I used to visit I took lentils because the little boy just loved scooping and pouring. One time he was enthusiastically pouring and laughing and as he did so he poured a huge scoopful out of the box and onto the floor. Since I knew Mum was very worried about mess I apologised profusely and started to scoop them up myself. Mum laughed, put her hand over mine and said: 'Just leave it. I'm used to you and I always clean up after you've gone now!'

When I was teaching, my assistants used to say that they dreaded coming in after the school holidays because they were always a bit unsure as to what new experience I would be introducing them to. The families of the children in my class were always excited at the new activities their children would be introduced to, but would not consider the possibility of doing the same activities in their own homes.

Therefore, as with all new ideas and experiences, you have to think about how everyone involved will feel. If you work in a family you have to think that you have been invited to work in their home and you have to treat everyone with respect and be guided by what they are comfortable with at the time. Most families I find start off really concerned, but once they witness the reactions of their children, they become more enthusiastic and want to do more. Some families have become messy play experts themselves and quickly want to share this with other families.

Planning the sessions

Here are some more pointers which should help your messy play sessions to go well.

STARTING OFF

When you start using messy play, start gently and build up in small stages. Don't go rushing in with tinned tomatoes on the first session! Messy play doesn't always have to be wet or food based, in fact in most situations it is best to start by using dry materials. You could begin with lots of shredded paper and then move on to sand and play dough.

MOVING ON

Once these have been shown to produce positive reactions and the family are in agreement you can move on to more wet materials. Again I would start with something safe such as cornflour and water, which will just brush away when dry. Then you can have more of an adventure and progress to condensed milk and maybe eventually the tinned tomatoes. I can see that you are worried about my obsession with tinned tomatoes, and I'll share my reasons later.

However, in all that you do first and foremost it *must be fun*! Yes we want the child to learn but it has to be fun at the same time. It's a time to play, explore and enjoy – both for you and the child. If you are worried or anxious about an activity, then the child will be worried too. On the other hand, if you are relaxed, happy and enthusiastic, then the child is more likely to be. Children and families, in fact everyone, learn best when they are having fun.

HICCUPS ALONG THE WAY

There will always be times when things don't go as well as you would want them to – that's life! If the activity is not fun and it is clear that no one is enjoying himself or herself, then it is best to stop. My advice for these occasions is to go back to the previous successful messy play experience and stay there for a while. Have some more successes with that activity before trying to move on into new things. After a number of successful experiences, when confidence has been rebuilt both for you, the child and the family, you can think about moving on again – perhaps in smaller steps or in a different direction altogether.

CHANGING DIRECTION

If you do decide to try a new direction, don't leap onto a very new and different experience, try and find something that is similar to the successful one, then the transition may be easier. For example, moving from foamy cream to condensed milk will be easier than moving from rice pudding to baked beans because the smell of the two milk products is similar and so the change may be easier to accept.

EQUIPMENT TO USE

So if we want these sessions to go well, what should we do? Well there is always a list of essential equipment to take with you, whether in the home or in the classroom. My list of essential equipment would be:

- a large clear plastic sheet (available cheaply from a camping supplies shop)

- wet wipes to clean the child's hands while Mum gets a bowl of clean water, otherwise you have the rice-pudding-in-the-hair-and-on-your-trousers experience!

- lots of containers to put the messy substance in when presenting it to the child; these would include flat trays, plastic pizza trays, ice-cream tubs, margarine tubs, etc.

- a large mirror – it can be exciting for the child to see herself as she plays with the messy substance and using this adds a visual dimension to the experience

- a piece of perspex – this enables the child to lie under it and watch the mess moving around

- a bowl and some soap for hand and face washing

- a towel

- rolls of cheap wallpaper – for putting the mess on or for painting and sticking

- laminate pockets – the messy substance can be put in these then squeezed around

- aprons for the child and any adults present – mainly this is for the family's peace of mind rather than the child, because the child usually would not think to wear it (I have learnt on many occasions that an overall for yourself is useful. Sometimes white is not a good colour to wear on a day when you are planning to do messy play activities. But if you should forget this you will be glad to have the overall.)

- a tin opener – you would not believe how many people do not have these and with ring pulls being quite readily available on named brand goods some would say you don't really need them; unfortunately I only use the cheap tinned goods and they don't have ring pulls!

- a large enamelled or non-stick square baking tray on which to place the mess – especially for those children who cannot lift their arms over a sided tray

- a large cat litter tray (new of course!) which is just the size and depth to use for large quantities of messy play

- two washing-up bowls – great for passing mess from one place to another and also good if you wish to have one wet and one dry container of the same substance

- some scoops or serving spoons (it's always best to have your own)

- a small dustpan and brush to clean up spills

- a large plastic bag to take away all the rubbish

- appropriate seating – where necessary.

EVALUATION

Messy play is usually used as a stepping stone towards achieving a long-term and significant goal. Evaluating or thinking what was good and what was bad about each session or experience is really important if the overall aim is to be achieved. You need to be honest about what happened, don't say it was good if it was awful. Sometimes you may need to persevere and repeat the experience a few times before the child comes to accept and enjoy it. Sometimes you might just need to accept that it didn't work and try something totally different next time. Don't be afraid of trying something again at a later date if you think that the experience was introduced too early. Remember that progress is often achieved small step by small step not as 'one giant leap for mankind'!

If you are always well prepared, know where you are going and what you want to achieve then you will be successful and messy play will be a beneficial experience for everyone. Remember there's a lot to think about before you start and that you need a lot of patience to do this and get it right, but don't be afraid to experiment and to learn as you go along.

And above all... *have fun!*

Part Two

BENEFITS OF MESSY PLAY

4 SENSORY STIMULATION

Every day of our lives all our senses are in continuous operation. From the moment we awake each morning to the moment we go to sleep we continually use and rely on the information they give us. The information collected will be about ourselves, our feelings, our bodies and how comfortable they are, the people we are with, the pets we have, our friends or work colleagues, the people who walk by on the pavement or sit next to us at work, the objects which form the environment of which we are part and the smells and sounds which come our way. Even when we are asleep and not consciously aware of them, our senses continue to operate, giving us a constant stream of data about our environment and circumstances, and if necessary an 'alarm call' to waken us to consciousness if there is threat or danger.

Our senses help us to find out about the world around us and to make sense of it. In many cases their operation is primarily to enable us to live safely, but often the senses operate purely for our pleasure and the enrichment of our lives. Without the ability to use our senses most of us would be lost or would find life very challenging indeed!

How would we enjoy our food if we did not have our senses of taste or smell? It has been shown that when one loses one's sense of smell, such as the times when one has a really heavy cold, the sense of taste disappears as well. The really spicy chilli we enjoy so much becomes bland and uninteresting if we cannot smell or taste it. If the heavy cold were to continue for an extended period of time, the experience of eating, which would normally provoke feelings of excitement and anticipation, becomes merely a chore and just something that you have to do.

Simple tasks become so much more difficult and potentially dangerous when we do not or cannot use our senses: crossing the road, choosing clothes, listening to instructions, being able to complete a task all become so much more complicated when one or more of our senses are lost.

However, think how it must be never to have been aware of our senses, never to have had the chance to use our senses. How would this affect us? How would we make sense of anything with which we came into contact?

THE SENSES

It is generally accepted that we have five senses:

- sight
- hearing
- touch
- taste
- smell.

However, more recently it has also been considered that we have two more:

- vestibular
- proprioceptive sense.

These senses are generally considered to be the inner senses. The vestibular sense helps us to process sensory information, which relates to the pull of gravity on the centre of the body and gives a sense of balance, speed and direction. The proprioceptive sense enables us to have an awareness of the position of the body in space, e.g. sitting, standing, lying.

These two senses need to work in co-ordination with the other five senses. It is input from the normal five senses which helps these additional or inner senses to mature. Every time that we change our position, for example from sitting to standing, then the parts of the inner ear and muscles and joints which help us to balance, cause the muscles in the body to make sure that the position is held securely so that we do not fall over. Thus children are developing these senses every time they move and fall over, and as they mature these senses develop alongside the traditional five. This can be seen especially through the visual sense and its interaction with the inner senses, which helps these inner senses to develop. Each time a child moves or is moved, his view of his surroundings changes and he uses his visual skills to understand where he is in relation to the world around him. From this information and that provided by his other senses he will be satisfied or dissatisfied with his new position and will feel comfortable or uncomfortable with it. If he is dissatisfied and uncomfortable, then he will wish to adjust his position to one more to his liking, and clearly this will need to be achieved before the child will wish to concentrate on any specific activity.

A normal healthy child will be born with all of these senses in place and fully operational. As the child grows and becomes more able to process and respond to the information given by the senses, so the child's ability to use them will also grow and develop. An example of this might be the development of the child's motor skills, which start as general arm movements then progress to specific movements to pick up a toy or object and later develop to the level of dexterity to make model aeroplanes or play a musical instrument.

However, when a child has a physical disability or a problem with one of the five senses, his ability to receive information through that sense is either lost or hindered. As a result of this it will be a lot harder for that child to make sense of the world around him and that is an area where messy play can be very helpful. However, before we look at this perhaps it would be helpful to look at how the senses develop.

Sight

It need hardly be said that vision is one of the most important senses for handling the world around us.

Even in the womb it has been noted that the foetus is sensitive to light. Lennart Nilsson noted in his book *A Child Is Born* (1990) that if a doctor looked inside the womb of a mother halfway through her pregnancy with a foetoscope which had a light source attached, then the foetus would try to shield its eyes with its hands.

Newborn babies focus on faces. They are fascinated by them, and given a choice between a plain colour and a face they will look at the face. They also like black and white colours, and later on simple repetitive patterns and then the colour red. Having learnt to look and focus on faces the baby then learns to concentrate on and track objects by following them with her eyes. Then gradually she begins to follow objects further away.

It is her visual skills that allow a child to develop the cognitive ability of *object permanence* – that a person or object has not gone away just because it cannot be seen any longer.

Vision also develops her perceptions of herself in relation to the world around her. For example, sight helps her to know how far away she is from an object so that she can reach out and grab it without falling over. Sight also helps her in her perception of size, shape, colour, height and depth, and in her ability to co-ordinate what she sees with what she does with her hands.

Hearing

The sense of hearing also develops well before birth. Foetuses can hear from within the womb, and it has been noted that the foetus reacts to sounds from five months gestation. The foetus recognizes its own mother's voice, familiar sounds in the home, such as the vacuum cleaner or the washing machine, or even a regular television theme, such as *Neighbours*. Babies have been noted to react positively to the music of Mozart. My niece Lisa used to calm to the sound of the Jon and Vangelis song *I'll Find My Way Home*. She could have been screaming for hours, but once that was played she calmed immediately; her mum and dad used to call it 'Lisa's magic music'. My own daughter Jess heard an awful lot of Michael Bolton's music when she was in the womb; it was the only thing that would calm her when she was a tiny baby.

Newborn babies can be startled by excessively loud or unfamiliar noises. They will cry in response to this unpleasant stimulation and throw out their arms and legs in a reflex action known as the Moro reflex. As they grow they become more accustomed to sounds such as the voice tones of their mother and their immediate family. They will look towards a familiar noise and will follow a sound as it moves, especially if they can see an object or person which moves to accompany it. They will also quieten to a soothing sound, and this can become the beginnings of a familiar routine associated with sleeping or, much later, bedtime.

The children then move on to other familiar sounds in their environment, such as a vacuum cleaner or the washing machine. Then they will begin to discriminate between sounds and start to associate them with the objects or people to which they relate. Then they begin to locate sounds further away.

The sense of hearing will also enable a child's language to develop, and the child will begin to make sounds and take turns in conversations, e.g. baby gurgles, Mum speaks, baby gurgles and Mum speaks. As time passes the baby will extend her range of sounds and start to differentiate some of the variety of sounds in the speech of her mother and others around her. At this stage it will often be the sound of the voice that conveys basic meaning rather than the specific words used. As more time goes by, the child begins to understand sounds and those sounds make words and those words have meaning and eventually she understands speech and is able to speak herself.

Touch

Touch is a vital sense for us all – even though most people do not really consider it at all. However, it should be remembered that the skin is the biggest organ of the human body and that it is full of sensory receptors. In light of this fact, perhaps we should be more aware of our sense of touch and how important it is for us. Certainly for children in the early stages of their lives, the sense of touch a very important means for the child to find out and make sense of the world around him.

Even from before birth the child is using his sense of touch. I have seen this in my own twins. They were fraternal but in the womb laid head to toe and would have felt each other at their feet. When they were born the first thing they did when lying in their cot was to touch each other's faces. As they grew older, they each slept with a soft toy between their ankles which I was told by the doctors and midwives was because they had been used to feeling each other in the womb.

Once born the child begins to explore and touch with his own hands and body. It is the means by which the child finds out about his own body, his mum and other members of his immediate family. Later this develops to his exploring his clothes, coverings, toys and eventually his food. This need to explore and to touch and feel everything with which he comes into contact is very important, as it is the way he finds out and understands his world.

Touch is also the sense that helps to keep him safe from harm in knowing hot and cold and pain. When he touches something hot, his sense of touch and the body's ability to register what we as adults would call pain enables the child to move away quickly from the source of harm. This sense, with the self-preservation it enables, is something that perhaps we do not acknowledge quite so much when we are grown up.

Consider then the example of a person suffering from leprosy. This is a disease that we fortunately do not experience in this country, but in some less developed countries it is something which, sadly, still exists. There is a tendency to believe that leprosy is a biblical problem, which need not concern us, but it is when one understands leprosy that one understands why touch is so important. Leprosy is a disease that attacks the nerve endings in the body. When leprosy is mentioned, pictures of people with fingers and toes missing may emerge. However, leprosy does not make fingers and toes drop off, it is the lack of feeling in these appendages which cause the problem. If you cannot feel whether something is hot or cold, then when you pick up a hot saucepan you won't drop it immediately because of the pain, because there is no sensation of pain. Fingers and toes are lost because they get damaged not because they are diseased.

This is just one example that demonstrates the importance of touch. It is a sense that we all need whether we are young or old. I would challenge anyone to tell me that clean sheets, a warm bath or holding another person's hand would be as delightful if the sense of touch had been damaged. The smells and sounds and sights of these experiences would still exist but without experiencing through touch, some of the perception of that experience would be impaired. Touch is indeed a vital sense.

Taste

Like touch, this is probably again a sense which is ignored unless we encounter circumstances in life when it ceases to function properly. In the womb babies practise swallowing the amniotic fluid from the age of three months. When born, the baby immediately begins to use her sense of taste when feeding. Whether breast or formula milk, the baby is using her taste buds to experience the milk. With breast milk the baby will also taste some of the foods that the mother eats.

The baby matures and begins to experience more tastes, moving on to some cereal foods and then gradually other tastes as a wider range of foods are introduced. Like all of us, the baby can show a preference for sweeter foods and will demonstrate a desire to eat some foods rather than others. However, a wide variety of foods is important if a child is to experience a full range of gustatory encounters.

Who can doubt that taste is important? Just imagine eating a chilli without the experience of the delicate balance of spices playing on your tongue, or chocolate without that soothing melting, sweet, rich taste. It would not be so interesting or enjoyable and eating would become just a mechanical necessity.

Smell

Smell is once again an undervalued sense and, as with the other senses, one does not really appreciate it until it has gone. It works hand in hand with the sense of taste – it has been shown on many occasions that without the sense of smell, it is very difficult to taste anything.

Remember when you last had a really heavy cold and you could not breathe through your nose. Not only was it incredibly difficult to breathe, but also it was difficult to eat with a closed mouth because you were trying to breathe through your mouth. Then as you are tucking into a long-awaited curry with a delicious hot chocolate fudge brownie with extra cream, you realize suddenly that you can neither taste nor smell anything. What should have been a spicy, pungent yet fragrant curry, and a wonderful chocolatey smelling dessert suddenly becomes a bland, tasteless mush. Eating becomes simply a mechanical task that has to be done. Remember this is only temporary; once the cold has followed its course you will regain your sense of smell and taste, and food and flowers and perfumes will again become a wonder for you.

However, imagine how this would be if it were to be permanent, if your sense of smell was permanently damaged. What if you have never experienced the fragrant smell of a rose, buried your face in the smell of clean washing, stood outside on a summer day and inhaled the smell of freshly cut green grass? How much would your experience and also most importantly your memories be affected?

Smell is one of the senses often associated with memories. We build up memories pleasant or otherwise in response to the experiences we take part in throughout our lives. We can remember a beautiful sunset or maybe a song and associate these with a particular place or event. However, I believe that smell can conjure up not only a memory of the smell but also a linked sight and a sound. A smell can also produce a memory that can transport a person back in his or her mind to the exact place and time that the smell was experienced.

For example, when I smell bacon cooking, I immediately remember camping holidays with my parents, glorious sunny days, horses in the fields nearby and the sound of birds in the bushes next to us. All of that from one smell!

When my daughter Sarah was born, she went into shock and spent a week in special care. I did not see her or hold her for two days because I was poorly as well. However, the nurses in intensive care gave me a blanket which I rubbed all over me and which they placed in Sarah's little greenhouse (actually her clear plastic hospital cot) with her. This was to help her get used to my smell and to recognize that smell on me when I was able to visit her and so help to reduce the possibility of her rejecting me. It worked!

On a more practical note, the remembrance of smell and its association with a particular person is the reason I always wear the same perfume when I visit my families. If the child has impairment to her sight or hearing, she will always know it is me because of my perfume.

The nose is not the only organ involved in the sense of smell. Behind the bridge of the nose is an organ known as the olfactory bulb which gathers all the smells. The signals are then sent along the olfactory nerve into the brain in the frontal lobes where the smell is interpreted and then stored in the memory. Therefore, if the brain, the nose or the olfactory bulb is damaged then the sense of smell will be affected. The part of the brain that deals with smell is the olfactory cortex. It is here that the brain co-ordinates the smell with pictures and sounds to provide lots of memory associations. The child's olfactory bulb acts almost like the retina in the eye: it is a receptor for the smell. As the child experiences more smells she begins to make associations with the smell and develop a smell bank linked to experiences in the brain. As the olfactory system is constantly updating itself then the smell banks grow.

Sensory Impairment

In the time that I have been working with children who are experiencing some form of sensory impairment, I have found that messy play has a valuable role. It is by focusing on the senses that the child can begin to learn more about the world in which he lives and start to develop a greater ability to understand and interact with it. As he does this, he discovers that things can be wet, dry, hot, cold, sticky, thick, thin, transparent, iridescent, pale, bright, shiny, sweet, sour, pungent, fragrant, and so on.

I would imagine that many people would say that this would occur without messy play. However, I do feel that in children who have more profound and multiple support needs this would not happen without the sensory activities being brought to them.

It is also the case that in the technical society we live in today, where the television and the computer have great importance, children can miss out on these vital sensory experiences because these activities are not accessed. They are used to the stimuli coming to them and then processing them, but until smelly vision or the television envisaged in Roald Dahl's *Charlie and the Chocolate Factory*, *where the watcher can reach in and grab and taste what is being shown, has been invented, then I do feel that children are missing out on the development of their senses if they only have 'passive' entertainment to stimulate them. This is especially true in younger children, because these closer senses develop earlier than the more distant ones.*

If there is a developmental problem with the senses, children will have to be taught to use them, just as they have to learn other abilities. It has been noted by several researchers that children move through a familiar sequence when learning about new experiences. The stages in this sequence are:

- awareness – reacting to a stimulus by chance or deliberately (e.g. wave an onion under a child's nose and he might pull away)

- attention – looking at and focusing on the stimulus

- localization – finding the stimulus by sight, sound, touch

- discrimination – knowing that a stimulus is the same as or different from another

- recognition – remembering smell, sound, touch (i.e. responding positively to a repeated stimulus)

- comprehension – responding to a stimulus by relating to previous experience.

Remembering this sequence can be helpful when engaging in messy play. The child may not immediately engage with the activity, but if you look carefully you may see that he is demonstrating one part of the learning experience. Once this has been identified, you can think in a more focused way about planning activities that will move him on to the next stage.

With children who have sensory impairments, you may have to think longer about how the messy play is presented. For example, you may not want to have too many colours of play dough on the table at the same time, or too many differing sounds or too many smells or tastes. While it may seem good to us to bombard the senses with all these stimuli, it might just produce an 'overload' response in the child, who could just switch off because there are too many sensations to process and she cannot differentiate between them.

Some points to consider:

- Try presenting only one smell, taste, sight, sound at a time.

- When appropriate ensure that there is no distracting background noise. (When I was a teenager I used to be able to read, study and do my homework all to the dulcet tones of Sting and the Police and an accompanying television programme, but now I find that is impossible – perhaps my processing systems are not working so well as before!)

- How is the child feeling in himself? A child who is unwell is less likely to be able to focus on activities than one who is well. A child also needs to feel safe in his environment and with the people in it in order to learn.

- Make sure that everyone is in a position where they can access the play easily.

- Remember that the close senses (touch, taste and smell, the vestibular and proprioceptive) develop earlier than the distance senses (sight and hearing). This is because the information gained through the close senses comes from direct contact, and the information gained through the distance senses comes through less direct contact. Therefore, activities requiring the close senses will probably have greater and more immediate success in younger children than those which require engagement of the distance senses.

- Hand over hand is not always a useful approach, especially if a child is tactile defensive. No child should be physically forced to explore anything as that will just cause withdrawal. In such cases, hand under hand may be considered where the child's hand rests on the adult's hand and the child experiences the activity through the movements of the adult's hand. The adult's hand is gradually removed over a period of time until the child is experiencing the activity himself. This step in itself may be something which takes a long time.

Example

I have been working recently with a boy who is extremely tactile defensive. I have been working with him now for 18 months and he is just about to move on to a pre-school setting. When I began to play with him he would not touch anything and would not allow me to use my hand over his hand to engage in an activity. It really has been back to the drawing board with this one. I began with plain, dry activities but he was even reluctant to try these.

His parents and I decided that we would use other implements that he could use himself to explore the activities. We have used wooden spoons, plastic and metal spoons, large and small spoons, scoops, spades and jugs. I have varied the activities through dry, to dry textured and wet smooth to wet textured. For a few weeks he has been playing with a box of thick split lentils, in which rubber snakes and lizards were hidden. When he first found them he immediately drew his hands away and pushed away the box, but in the last few weeks he has been touching the lentils with his fingertips and allowing his family to pour them into his hands. He also began to ask for them using his own sign of rubbing his fingers together.

In my final visit I took with me some play snow. This looks like snow, feels wet and cold like snow but when your hand is removed it is dry. He pushed it away at first, but then watched as I poured it into the tray from above him. Then he watched as I caught it in my hands. He then decided to use a spoon and scoop it and, while I was not watching, tentatively touched the snow with his fingertips. After ten minutes he was fully exploring the snow by himself and laughing. That was success but it was a long time coming!

From this example we can learn that:

- activities may need to be repeated in order for the child to co-ordinate the information brought through his senses with his motor, thinking and communication skills

- sometimes you need to give space for the child to explore on his own

- you may also have to allow time for a response to be made.

When you consider all these things, it is amazing that we develop as we do almost innately. Understanding how our senses develop and operate can help us to consider how and when messy play can be used most successfully, although, as stated before, results may not always be immediate.

WE WENT TO FRANCE FOR THE DAY

As a teacher of children with additional support needs I was given many exciting and unusual things to do in order to extend the experiences of the children. It was decided that it was vital for the children to learn a foreign language. This was a very difficult thing to contemplate as the majority of the children in my class were non-communicative and with a very poor level of understanding. We knew we had to do something and so we decided as a class that we would have a 'day trip to France'. We would immerse the children in France and its culture. We would provide a multisensory experience!

We began by changing the classroom and filling it with colours of red, white and blue. We hung large French flags in the room, and parents sent their children in dressed in stereotypical French clothing – one little boy even had a rather large Eiffel Tower hanging around his neck! We decided that we would have a French breakfast, and so the children arrived to the wonderful smell of hot croissants, hot chocolate, freshly baked French bread and coffee.

Then there was a wonderful tasting session, which the children loved, and also some lovely messy play involving sticky chocolate. We also assaulted their ears with varying French tunes and spoke simple French phrases accompanied by familiar Makaton signs throughout the day. This was our answer to the foreign language problem and it was rather successful.

After this successful activity, multisensory activities became the order of the day. I remember that we were looking into the weather, especially rain. We changed the classroom into a rainy area with strips of green and blue crepe paper hanging down from the ceiling, so that every time a child passed through the classroom he felt the paper tapping on him rather like raindrops. We used a lot of water coloured blue for pouring and splashing, and bubbles which when popped on arms and legs again felt like raindrops.

We also engaged in some very messy bubble painting. This culminated in a day when we had planned that the children, dressed for rain and under umbrellas, would experience the rain. However, the best-laid plans of mice, men and Tracey never result as they should. It was a sunny day all day. This meant a sudden change of plans. It was too hot for rain macs but we still put the children in wellies and then placed their feet in bowls of water and splashed their feet (as if they were splashing in puddles). Therefore they enjoyed the splashing, wet feeling and heard the sound. Then we placed them under large fishing umbrellas, attached a hose to a tap, passed the hose out of the window, turned the water on and sprayed the umbrellas, all the time shouting 'It's raining!' It was a wonderful and very memorable experience.

I know that this type of multisensory activity would be impossible in the home or in a group, but some of the ideas could be used to create a great experience which would stimulate the senses.

You could use bowls of different coloured water for splashing and pouring, blowing 'Touchabubbles', which are a special type of bubble that do not pop immediately and can be stacked and touched before they can be popped. A large bowl of soapy water full of bubbles could also be used to give the dropping sensation of rain on skin when they pop. The French experience could be repeated with bowls of blue, red and white paint and cooked spaghetti.

You could also make up a bowl of cornflour and water and add coffee to give smell and colour. This could also be carried out with chocolate flavouring to give a rich chocolatey smell. Perhaps this might be considered to be stereotyping France, perhaps it is, but it is an experience.

It should also be remembered that even when focusing on one sensory activity in messy play, all the senses come into to play in order to take part in that activity. For example, you might be using orange jelly. This stimulates visual senses because it is such a bright colour, its strong orangey smell will stimulate smell while at the same time stimulating taste – the salivary glands will begin to work in anticipation of the taste – hearing will be promoted by the sloppy sounds and burping noises that jelly always seems to make, together with the watery sounds it makes as it melts. Finally it will also bring into play the tactile sense when the child begins to feel and explore the jelly with his hands or feet.

It is so easy to think that you are going to focus just on one sense, but because all senses seem to work together to provide a person with a wonderful three-dimensional experience and understanding of any given situation, I do not think that you can isolate any one of them. Even with sensory impairment of one or even two senses, the remaining three or four will still be working together, no one sense works on its own.

The example of Helen Keller is a good one to use here. She was a child who became blind and deaf and then mute after an illness. She had lost two of her senses and could not make sense of the world around her and became quite uncontrollable. Her parents asked for help from Thomas Edison; he introduced them to a teacher named Annie Sullivan, who was blind herself. She then taught Helen to use her other senses in order to make sense of the world around her. She taught her finger spelling by spelling the word in the palm of her hand. The noted breakthrough was water being poured into Helen's hand while Annie was spelling out the word 'water' on her palm. Helen grabbed Annie's palm and spelt 'water' and then immediately began to want to know more words. She learnt to speak by feeling the vibrations on Annie's throat and eventually learned to read using Braille. Smell and taste would also have been involved and working at the same time to help develop a greater understanding.

This is a good example of how the interaction and stimulation of other senses can help to compensate for the loss or partial loss of one or more senses.

SENSORY PLAY: SOME EXAMPLES

Jelly

I'm sure by now that everyone thinks that all I use is jelly. I admit I do use a lot of jelly, because it is so versatile. It is really cold and yet it can also be quite warm. It can come in granules or blocks. It can be used in a small container, or a larger container can be filled with jelly for a wonderful group, social experience. Jelly can also come in small pots which can be tipped out and used for squeezing and poking. These are good examples for developing hand skills, while at the same time stimulating smell, sight, sound and touch.

You can also hide objects in jelly and use this in a more advanced programme, possibly the later stages when working with someone who is tactile defensive. The wonderful smell can encourage even the most reticent child to want to explore.

Custard powder

I'm sure lots of you have mixed cornflour and water and made 'gloop', that wonderful stuff which changes before your eyes from a solid to a liquid. There is even a scientific name for that amazing process – blend morphology! However, although it is great to explore it also has a smell which is not particularly nice and can prevent children from wanting to engage with the activity.

To overcome this, I have found that custard powder is a great replacement. It has the same properties as the cornflour and water, but it is bright yellow and has a wonderful smell.

Banana milkshake

I am told by the scientists that banana has a chemical in it called amyl acetate and it is this which gives bananas and pear drops their strong and distinctive smell. I would also warn that these smells can be pleasant to some people but to others they can produce some negative reactions. My friend cannot bear bananas, just sitting next to someone who is eating one can cause her great discomfort. This really is a smell where you need to check for allergies or adverse reactions before embarking on its use.

I have used bananas regularly with the children I have worked with. My own children ate bananas as a staple part of their diet when they were younger – perhaps that is why some of them don't like to eat them any more.

When I was teaching, banana milkshake was a great favourite for messy play. It would be used as a group activity and we would place the granules on the table and add little amounts of water, enough to make a thick sticky mixture. We would encourage the children to explore with their hands and make movements and patterns. Then we would place sugar paper on top and take prints. These mountainous pieces of art we would hang on the wall, and as they dried they gave off a wonderful banana odour and once dry felt amazing if you ran your hands over them.

However, I have had one occasion using banana milkshake which was not quite so successful. I was working with a little boy who was learning to point and explained to his parents that banana milkshake mixed thickly would be a great medium to use for some pointing work. Mum and Dad thought it was a great idea and were very excited when I arrived with the materials on a Monday morning.

With the young man ready in his chair, we opened the milkshake box. The little boy made a slight gagging sound. I asked Mum and Dad if he was fine and they assured me he was and that I should carry on. I tipped the powder into a large bowl and placed it in front of him; he gagged again. Once again I asked Mum and Dad if he was fine and once again they said to continue. Then I added the water, at which point the young man vomited in the bowl! Needless to say we stopped at that point! Mum and Dad said that he had never reacted in that way before and they were very surprised.

On the basis of that experience I am a little more wary of banana and banana milkshake now and check with parents very carefully before using it.

Tinned tomatoes and baked beans

These are also wonderful to use for sensory stimulation. Again they can be used on a one-to-one basis in a shallow tray, but can also be used as a group activity if placed in a large tray that all the children can stand around or straight onto a table to explore.

Tinned tomatoes and baked beans have the potential to stimulate all the senses. They are a bright red colour, they have a pungent odour, they feel amazing – especially if you use whole plum tomatoes and squeeze them in your hands so that the seeds pop out! They also make interesting sounds and have quite a sweet taste.

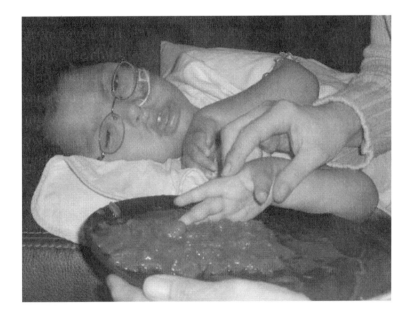

I could go on and give many more examples here, but I am going to cover these in future chapters and I don't want to repeat myself. Therefore, for more examples please look in the later chapters about dry play, wet play, non-messy play and pre-writing skills.

5 LANGUAGE AND COMMUNICATION

DEVELOPMENT OF COMMUNICATION SKILLS

We are all born with a blank page as regards language and communication. It is as if we are waiting for someone or something to fill in and print the page or write the book. That makes it sound as if we are passive recipients just waiting for language and communication to be imprinted on us, and in some ways this is partly true. As babies we all move toward and attempt to interact with our environment and with people in that environment. Most of us are born with an innate ability to do that, but this is not so with all children. Those who have additional support needs are likely to need extra help to develop these skills. From my experience of working with these children, I believe, messy play can provide this help.

Language and communication skills begin to develop from birth. From the moment of arrival on planet earth, the baby begins to show a startle response to noises around him. He learns that if he makes a noise himself, something generally happens, for example he might be cuddled, fed or cleaned. As he grows, he learns that coos and gurgles are greeted with more sounds and smiles, and then he responds with a smile. Then the baby's focus of attention moves away from his carer and he becomes more interested in his environment. He demonstrates this by looking at objects around him and then reaching and grasping for them.

As he does this, his carer begins to name and talk about these things. The baby will continue to make more sounds in response to this and will gradually develop his understanding of his immediate world. He will make gestures, point at objects and will be rewarded by his carer naming them.

Then the baby will begin to form words from his sounds, at first in imitation and then with meaning and intent. Then as the child grows he progresses from single words carrying much meaning, to two-word utterances, and then developing grammar until eventually he can understand what is said to him and can carry out simple conversations.

All of this takes time and it is not until the child is about four years old that most of the speech and comprehension systems are fully developed and his speech will be fully understandable by strangers.

However, for language to develop there are some underpinning skills that need to develop first. These are such skills as:

- eye contact
- attention skills
- vision
- hearing.

If the development of any of these skills is delayed, then language and communication can be delayed. This does not necessarily mean delay only in speaking, but also in such things as ability to interact, use of gestures, ability to pretend and comprehension.

It is also important to note very clearly that all children are individuals and all children will develop at their own pace and not necessarily at the same pace as their peers. Whilst there is such a thing as 'normal development', we must also recognize that few children will fit the general pattern in all aspects. The pace of development in different areas will also be influenced by the child's position in the family in relation to her siblings and family environment and general circumstances.

Messy Play and Language and Communication

Although parents and professionals may have an agenda for the encouragement and development of the child's communication skills and can employ the use of strategically targeted activities through such schemes as the Derbyshire Language Scheme, the child will often respond more positively through the use of non-threatening play activities.

In making this distinction, I would not want you to believe that I feel there is no place for such specialist schemes. These schemes and step-by-step progressive activities are effective and do encourage communication extremely well. However, I would also say that play activities can sometimes give an opportunity to practise skills learnt in a less structured but equally effective way. This is where messy play activities can help.

It is always important to remember several things, which will encourage language and communication during a messy play session:

- Keep your language simple.

- Keep sentences short.

- Try commenting on what the child is doing rather than asking lots of questions, e.g. What's this? What are you doing? What's that? What does this do? This can sometimes lead to a child only ever hearing questions and then modelling this in his own speech. Try to use phrases like 'Joe's poking', 'Joe's blowing'.

- Model the same level of language as your child, e.g. if he uses one word, you use one word, etc.

- Use gestures or Makaton to accompany speech – a signing system used with speech – if appropriate.

- Respond immediately and positively to any communication attempts by the child.

- Always try to use eye contact when you talk to your child and make sure you get down to his level when you communicate with him.

- Singing is good, some children will respond better to singing than to speech.

Eye contact

This is a vital skill for language and communication. Messy play can happen anywhere – on a tray, in a bowl or as a group around a large water tray. It is always a good idea to sit opposite the child when engaging in play activities. This will enable you to take every opportunity to catch and positively react to any eye contact opportunity that presents itself. Make sure you move to the child and avoid moving the child himself. Another suggestion would be to imitate the movements of the child so that whatever the child does you will also do immediately.

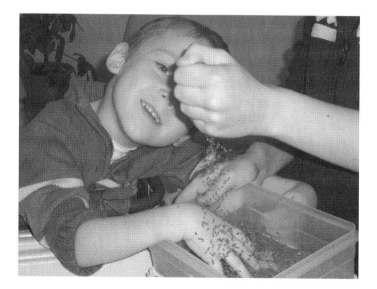

Waiting

This is also another skill important for language and communication development. Learning to wait to speak or waiting while you listen to someone else speak is a key skill in any conversation. In messy play the adult can perform a task or activity and then wait to see how the child will react. This gives the child an example to follow.

This can then be built on by encouraging the child to wait before he imitates an activity. The adult would perhaps say 'Wait' and sign the Makaton for wait, and after a short time then allow the child to play. Some 'Ready, steady, go!' games would also help this.

In the small group activities that I have been carrying out we always have a time of messy play. We use a lot of water wheels in our play and, whether pouring compost, coloured rice, lentils, water or custard, we hold a scoop above the wheel and say 'Ready, steady, go!' Then we wait for the children to make any kind of utterance before completing the task and pouring the media through the wheels.

We have also encouraged this by stirring the substances really quickly and then stopping and again saying 'Ready, steady, go!' then waiting again, and resuming stirring quickly again when the children start making sounds.

Taking turns

This builds upon the waiting skills mentioned above. Taking turns is a key skill and discipline to be observed in all social experiences. It is important to learn that we all share time and space with everyone else, and taking turns in play helps this to develop.

In messy play sessions the adult could engage with the substance and then turn to the child and say 'John's turn', and on that cue the child would take his turn to engage and play with the substance.

Once the child has grasped the skill and discipline of taking turns, this can be further extended to a group setting where the activity takes place around a large container and the child shares the activity with a number of other children or adults. In this context, each child or adult will need to take turns to experience the play. This skill would then be transferred to other settings such as playing games and taking turns to play with toys.

Concentration

Whilst this is difficult to explain from a theoretical point of view, from practice it just seems that the more that you engage in messy play with a child, the more the child's concentration span seems to increase. This is great news for the child and is key to many learning opportunities that will become available later on. As they grow, most children learn to concentrate and block out distractions when working on a task. Children with additional support needs will learn to do this too, but it will just take longer and be a more gradual progression.

I have found that it is best if you start doing messy play for short sessions and then, once the child is fully engaged and success starts to build, the duration of the session can be increased.

Copying

This is a parallel to mirroring the child's actions, which we covered in chapter 2. Copying happen very easily during messy play. The child can splash and then you can splash. The child can slap your hand with something sticky and then you can do the same. You can of course copy the sounds that the child makes during messy play, and this will encourage him to make further sounds. However, as with everything else, this does not happen automatically; it takes time and requires patience from the worker involved.

Your own responses to the child's activities will help in the success of this. I was using condensed milk with a child one day and I was

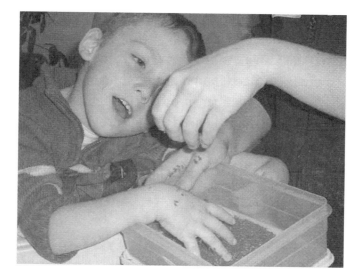

moving my hand round and round in the milk. As I did so I smeared some milk on the child's hand and continued moving the milk around. Then I repeated this again and again. After a while the child reached over and slapped my hand with the milk. At which point I made a rather exaggerated shriek and laughed. The child immediately did the same thing and, because I gave the same reaction, did it again. This was the beginning of his copying activities.

Sound making

This can be encouraged in many ways. Generally in messy play it is the precursors to speech that can be encouraged. This would include the development of basic skills such as blowing, sucking, licking and some chewing.

While playing with the messy substance you could also use and encourage some symbolic sounds, such as slurping, blowing bubbles, mmmm, yum yum, etc. Gestures, possibly based on the Makaton signing system, can also be encouraged, but these should always be accompanied by speech. The first and easiest one to use would be 'more' when encouraging the children to repeat an activity.

I am not saying that children will immediately start making sounds, gestures or speaking but the messy play activities, when carried out regularly and consistently, will stimulate this.

Singing

Singing is wonderful. Music seems to have a special power that I am not sure we really understand. Sometimes music can creep its way into a person and achieve results that nothing else can. There is so much documentation about music unlocking the most locked up persona.

When I was teaching there was a little girl in my class who was severely autistic and would scratch herself and pull her hair out. However, if music were played in the room, that little girl would calm down and almost seem to change and become someone else. The music certainly seemed to make a difference to her.

In messy play as in all activities, singing can be employed to accompany movement. Whatever you do, a song can be used to help this. It does not really matter what the tune is, it is the rhythm and rhyme which holds the key.

For example, I work with a little boy who is blind. He does not speak but seems to understand all that is said to him. Whatever we do, we sing; and I am finding that he is humming along perfectly in time and with the correct tone. When we play with water I will sing 'We are moving round and round, round and round, all day long' (to the tune of *The Wheels On The Bus*), or when we are pouring pasta I will sing 'Dave is pouring the pasta, pasta, Dave is pouring the pasta, look at him' (to the tune of Let's All Sing Together). You really do not have to be the world's best singer to do this, you just have to be enthusiastic and have fun!

Therefore you can see that messy play has its place in the encouragement of language and communication skills. At the risk of repeating myself, I must emphasize that this is not a miracle cure for all ills. It must be used alongside other strategies to reinforce skills learnt. Above all, messy play should be fun. So don't worry if you do not have the voice of an angel, your child will just enjoy being with you, sharing your attention and having fun!

6 SOCIAL DEVELOPMENT

DEVELOPMENT OF SOCIAL SKILLS

Everybody learns to become a social person from the moment they are born. A baby is born an individual and at first is only involved and interested in himself. As he develops, he gradually begins to interact with the world and others around him and starts to learn that he is not alone but part of a family unit and then a wider society. Along the way he will need to learn all the 'social airs and graces' that we, as adults, all understand.

The first thing that a baby learns is that when he makes a sound someone else will make the sound in return, that he can repeat the sound again and that the sound will in turn be repeated back to him. He will also learn that the human face is really interesting and that it makes lots of different actions and sounds. He will then look at any face which comes within the range of his vision, initially making good eye contact and then gradually extending this expressive repertoire to include smiles and more sounds.

Through this process, the baby is learning that he is not an individual and that he can encourage other people to respond to him through the use of his sounds and facial responses. From this, he then moves on to develop an understanding that he is his own person and that his body is his own body and that when he moves his body it is his body moving and not another person's. He learns that he can touch and feel his own body but not the feelings in another person's.

Later on, he also starts to understand that objects and people are always there even when they cannot be seen any more. This is something known as object permanence. Before this concept is understood, a baby will cry when Mum leaves the room because she believes that Mum has gone and is never coming back. After this concept has been grasped, she understands that Mum is still around somewhere even if she cannot be seen, and she has faith that she will return at some point.

Turn taking and copying also begins to be learnt. This begins with eye contact, smiles and sounds. The baby will learn that people smile at him and then he smiles back and they then smile again, and so on. This is a very basic turn taking which then moves on to turn taking in expressing sounds, then turn taking in word utterances before finally turn taking in sentences, which is the format of normal conversation. The development of this pattern in speech can then be transferred to play and other activities.

Babies also learn to copy others while they watch them. Babies learn that when they copy something that others do, it usually gains them approval from the other person. Everybody likes positive responses, and babies and children are no different. When they are praised for doing something good then they usually want to do it again to get praised again. This is where copying begins. Eventually the development of these social skills leads to a change in the style and scope of play activities.

LEARNING SOCIAL SKILLS THROUGH MESSY PLAY

When children start to play they play by themselves; this is called *solitary play*. As they begin to sit up and move around they continue to play by themselves but will tolerate playing next to another child, although they do not actually play with the other child. This is called *parallel play*. Then they start to watch the other child playing next to them. This is followed by joining in play, but only so much as it will benefit them. Finally they will play with each other, taking turns, copying and helping each other in play, and this is known as *co-operative play*.

All of this and much more can be learned through the medium of messy play. Messy play will also help to develop bonding and relaxing through close contact play. Messy play can be carried out alone, but it is much better and more beneficial if it is carried out with someone or in a group. Playing with another person encourages eye contact, skin-to-skin contact and feelings of togetherness.

An example of this happened the other day as I introduced chopped tinned tomatoes to a child and his family. The little boy was sitting in his chair and I placed the tomatoes in front of him. He looked at the tomatoes and then looked at me (eye contact). I smiled at him (eye contact). He looked at the tomatoes again and I pointed at them, smiled and said 'Ooh…tomatoes! Yummy!'

He looked at me again and then looked at Mum (eye contact). Mum said 'Tomatoes…Yummy Yummy!' and smiled. I took one finger, put it into the tomatoes and started to move it round in the tomatoes saying 'Round and round and round'.

He looked at me (eye contact) and then tentatively put one finger in the tomatoes and looked at me again (eye contact). Mum and I both smiled and said again 'Round and round yummy!' Then he put his whole hand in the tomatoes and I responded by copying him and doing the same. He said 'Roun…roun'. We all laughed and smiled at each other (eye contact).

Then getting braver I picked up the tomatoes and squeezed saying 'Squeeeezzzee!' Then, looking at him, I placed some in his hands and squeezed them through his fingers. He smiled and then slapped his hands down in the tomatoes. This resulted in tomatoes spraying all over me! I laughed and shouted in surprise (positive verbal feedback for him).

He looked at me again (eye contact) and slapped his hands down again, and again and again all the while getting wonderful responses from me (positive feedback for him) and looking intently at me (brilliant eye contact).

You can see from this example that there were some wonderful social responses and all through a tin of tomatoes! This was simple, inexpensive and messy, but so much fun!

The main thing about messy play, as I keep saying, is that it has to be fun. If something is fun and is not seen as threatening then the child and everyone else relaxes. This helps to maximize the potential benefit from the messy play activity and, among other positive benefits, helps in the development of social skills.

Another example of this comes to mind from working with the same little boy mentioned above who was actually tube fed, and at the time had been for the previous two years. Mum had expressed concern that he was not attempting to eat and seemed worried by food. This was possibly because the whole situation of food and eating had become tense, anxious and difficult and was not proving to be the happy, relaxing time that it should be.

We decided to engage in some messy play sessions to try and move things forward in this area of his development and we tried using condensed milk, custard and squirty cream. These had all been very happy, relaxed sessions and each time the little boy had explored more and more with the encouragement of his mum and dad, who had continued to use these activities in between my weekly visits. The family just had fun with food with no – or very few – worries about eating. This led to the little boy removing his tube himself, telling everyone 'tube gone' and beginning to eat and enjoy his food. I don't know for certain if it was messy play that helped this process but it may have reduced the pressure and brought back some fun into this key social situation and life skill.

Another little girl that I worked with had very little eye contact with either her parents or myself. As well as experiencing some more complex needs she also was hearing and visually impaired, and this all added to limiting her ability to interact with the world around her.

She was able to move around her environment backwards on her back and when something was placed in her hand she was able to hold it briefly. Sitting was quite difficult for her as she regularly pushed herself backwards. Therefore we decided to place her in her standing frame for her messy play sessions.

We began again by using condensed milk. Usually she would fling her head back, but as we helped her to bring her arms around to the front of the tray, she put her head down and began to inspect the milk. We placed her hands into it and moved them around. She did not pull back but allowed me to move her hands in it. It is very sticky and she began to smile and make sounds. She even began to squeeze it with her fingers and then as Mum sat in front of her she looked up and gave some good eye contact. We were all really pleased and Mum continued to use this all week and achieved some excellent results. We continued with our messy play sessions every week for at least six months, progressing from condensed milk to rice pudding, to lentils, to baked beans. Every time we used the messy play the little girl gave some good periods of eye contact, which Mum and Dad then found was also occurring outside the sessions. She had discovered that the response to her eye contact was so positive that she began to use it at other times and increasingly so as she enjoyed the positive reinforcements from Mum and Dad.

Another little boy – in fact, one of the first children that I started to do home visits with – was very mobile, very active and loved to play with toys by himself, but apart from Mum and Dad he would not allow anyone else to play either with him or nearby. He would also not give any eye contact, and Mum and Dad were finding that it was becoming really hard to communicate with him.

We began our sessions by using lentils – bright orange ones which really did catch his eye! I would place them in a big plastic tray with high sides and move my hands round and round and gradually encourage him to place his hands in the tray. Then I moved on to pouring the lentils onto his hands and eventually pouring them from above his head and he would try to reach for them. This was the most successful thing to do because as I did so I would say 'Ready…steady…GO!' and gradually he would watch me until I said 'GO!'

Then we moved on to using dried pasta. This was not only bigger but made a wonderful sound as it hit the tray and this created much laughter and eye contact. After this we moved onto jelly and Angel Delight, which were also really successful at promoting some excellent eye contact through pouring, and squashing in the hands. Using the Makaton sign for 'more' and asking 'Do you want more?' also encouraged him to look at me as I spoke.

This eventually led from eye contact to pointing, which neither his parents nor me expected that he would ever be able to do. Mum and Dad were so pleased because this allowed them to begin to communicate properly with their son for the first time. Now they could ask him what he wanted, they could offer a choice of photographs and their little boy would point at the chosen one and look at them as he did so. It enabled them for the first time to understand him, it gave him some element of choice in his life and the activities he wanted to do. And for them it was a real joy.

Copying

Imitating what another person is doing is an important skill in social development. Imitating the movements or sounds of another person shows that the child is interested in and aware of other people. Clapping and waving bye bye are skills that children initially enjoy copying and that can also be worked on through messy play.

Water and bubbles are excellent media for encouraging this. Of course this does mean that you and probably everyone else in the room will also become messy. In view of this, it's probably best to warn everyone in advance!

In a one-to-one situation, a bowl of warm soapy water can be placed in front of the child. The idea is that you then place your hands in the water and clap them together. Then you place the child's hands in the water and help him to clap his own hands together. Watch for any movement and then repeat. The bubbles are especially useful for gaining a positive response. The bubbles are soft, and 'ex-

plode' as they are clapped together. It becomes messier the more the child claps. It is a great activity.

A successful example of bubble play occurred with a boy that I met in one of the group situations run by my friend and colleague Julie. We were using a large water tray filled with bubbly coloured water. We had given the children straws and were encouraging them to blow bubbles in the water. One particular boy was very difficult to engage in the activities as he was easily distracted and would not remain at an activity for very long.

Using the straws we blew bubbles in the water and as we did so he began to look at the bubbles and then at us. His mum was thrilled as he had never done this before. She took this activity home and continued to use this with him at bathtime and found that his concentration, eye contact and turn-taking skills all improved.

This activity can also be carried out in a group situation. The children can be standing around a large water tray and this can be filled with water and bubbles. In this situation, once one child starts to clap, you will find that all the children will begin to clap in the water and lots of fun will ensue. A great deal of mess will be made as well so it would be good to use aprons with this activity!

Turn taking

Another social skill, which is vital to all children, is turn taking. This is also important in language development in that the children learn that each person takes turns in speaking. In playing with all the media, the children can learn to wait to carry out the activity and then take their turn saying 'your turn, my turn' and 'waiting'.

For example, you can pour pasta in to a tub and while you are doing this you can say 'Waiting' then give the child the pasta and say 'Your turn'. This activity can also be carried out in a group situation around a large bowl or in a home situation with the child and the parents taking turns. Once the child has learnt to take turns within the messy play situation then this new skill can be used in other situations. This is a great fun way to learn to take turns.

I hope you can see that messy play is a great means of aiding social skills development. Again I must emphasize that it should not be used on its own and should always be used with other activities so that the skills learned can be generalized to different situations. The development of social skills is vital to our ability to interact with the world. Without these skills it is difficult to do anything, because although we are all individuals separate from everyone else, it is also true that 'no man is an island' and that we need to interact with other people if our lives are to be fulfilling and satisfying.

7 MOTOR SKILLS

DEVELOPMENT OF MOTOR SKILLS

Motor skills are considered in two groups and these are:

- gross motor skills – to do with the co-ordination of major movements of either the whole body or of one or more arms or legs
- fine motor skills – to do with the co-ordination of smaller movements of hands and fingers.

When we undertake a task, both groups of skills are usually required, and normally the interaction between them is automatic and unconscious. For example, if we want to pick something up from a table, we will need gross motor skills to move our body and stretch out our arm until our hand is positioned slightly above the object. Then we will need to use fine motor skills to adjust the position of the hand and flex the fingers and thumb to grasp the object in the correct way and with the correct amount of pressure. Once the object has been grasped we will then use gross motor skills again to raise the arm and possibly our whole bodies to carry the object to where we want it to go. Releasing the object will require the use of fine motor skills again in order to place the object gently where we want it to be rather than drop it clumsily.

Each child develops these skills at his or her own pace. There are lots of assessment charts used to show how children develop and in which age range each activity should be expected, but it should always be remembered that they show age ranges within which a behaviour would be expected, not milestone days or dates. A child does not have to be immediately doing a specific skill just because he is two years old that day; it may take a few more months or even another year.

Development begins at the head and gradually moves down through the body to the feet. Therefore *gross motor skills* start to develop first with controlling movements of the head. Then the child will move to upper body control, such as pushing up with his arms while on his tummy and then rolling over. Next he will learn to sit up and from here he will learn to crawl. Starting from a sitting position, he will move onto all fours, then rock, then reach out with one hand in the crawl position, then crawl.

Once this has been mastered, the child will then learn to stand with support and then stand alone, reach out to grasp something in front of him, then take a few steps and then walk. He will also learn to stand up from sitting and sit from standing and stoop to pick something up and return to standing. Then he will learn to run, hop, jump, throw and catch. He will also learn to climb up and then down. As the child grows the movements become more complex and sophisticated as the child gains more control over his body.

Fine motor skills develop first with eye control and then hand-eye co-ordination. For example when a child is looking at an object that is moving from one side of his vision to the other, he will move his eyes so as to keep the object in view. If this become impossible or uncomfortable to achieve with just eye movements, he will move his head as well. This same skill operates when the object makes a sound and is moving from one side of him to the other. In this situation he will again move his head in order to keep the sound in focus and 'follow' it.

After he has learned to follow or track objects or sounds, he will move on to learn to reach out and grasp an object which is offered to him. His grasp will then develop gradually from a whole hand grasp to a finer grasp with three or two fingers and then an ability to move the object around in the hand.

The child will then learn to hold two objects at the same time with one in each hand, then how to bang them together and then will move on to use both hands to carry out activities such as twisting, pulling and pushing, dressing and undressing, using a tool in her hand (e.g. scissors or putting beads on a thread). This will in turn lead on to pencil control.

MOTOR SKILLS TRAINING THROUGH MESSY PLAY

Messy play can be used in to encourage motor skill development. Mainly I use it for assisting in fine motor skill development, but I have also used it for gross motor skill development.

As stated previously, messy play has always been a big part of the life of my own children. We used messy play from a very young age, almost as soon as they could be propped up in a high chair. We were fortunate to have a large kitchen-diner in our first home and so the children were always with me in the kitchen.

At first, they were in a playpen and watched my activities from behind bars! Then they moved into a bouncy chair on the floor, and I brought the activity down to them, mostly in the form of a bowl full of bubbly water or a bowl of flour. Once they could sit propped up they went into a high chair, and then the possibilities were endless!

We would cook together, feeling and tasting all the ingredients and stirring the mixture round and round in a mixing bowl, at first hand over hand and then as fine motor skills progressed, by themselves. I have five children, so at some point I had five children of varying abilities in the kitchen all experiencing messy cooking each in their own way. When I began to look after a little girl with cerebral palsy as a respite carer, she too joined our merry band in the kitchen.

Once the children were walking we moved on to messy play in the garden. I remember one incident in the middle of February when my twins wanted to be in the garden. They went out wrapped up in wellies and duffle coats, but soon wanted the sandpit open. Not filled with sand – no, they wanted it filled with cold water. Instead of wanting to wear their wellies, they wanted bare feet! They learnt a lot that day. They learnt to balance on a slippery surface. They learnt to stand on one leg because their feet were so cold, they could not have both feet in the water at the same time! They also learnt to pour water from a height and fill up containers until they were full, as well as stepping up and down out of the sandpit. It was great fun and an amazing day!

Of course, messy play would not be complete in our family without venturing into mud and dirt in the garden. My son was always fond of digging and used to spend hours digging under a fir tree which stood at the bottom of the garden. He loved getting messy and he loved the joy of digging to try and find something. In doing this he was using his gross motor skills to do the digging and his fine motor skills in searching through the mud and dirt to find 'great archaeological discoveries', such as the long-lost dead dog which – we presume – had been buried there by the previous owners!

Sarah, one of my twins, was always fascinated by the great outdoors. Wherever we went she would be stooping down on the ground making mud pies and creating structures like something out of the film *Close Encounters*, with sand, leaves or the bark chippings in playgrounds. It was a wonderful sensory experience for her and encouraged her to use her fine motor skills.

Another tendency in our family was to use vast quantities of paint. My husband was always uncertain what he would find when he came home from work. We painted pictures on the windows with brushes and our hands! We made handprints, feet prints, welly prints – we even painted our bodies and made giant body prints! We had such fun! And all the while the children were learning so much. My children will tell you that these times were the ones that gave them the best memories of being children.

Now I am not suggesting that giant body prints might be something that could be employed in a professional setting. I am trying to show from my own experience that messy play can be used at all stages to encourage development in gross and fine motor skills.

Some play ideas

Play dough and cooked spaghetti in paint is wonderful for encouraging squeezing and releasing! It feels wonderful to do this, but sometimes it also feels so awful that it really does encourage a good release. Jelly is also excellent for this. Pouring tapioca over a closed hand can also encourage that hand to open, and pouring it over an open hand can also encourage closure.

Standing in a group around a big tray full of some really sticky, messy medium such as wet porridge oats or mashed potato, or even pasta and glitter, promotes excitement and this activity can encourage a child to take his weight and stand in order to join in rather than remain sitting and possibly be left out of the activity.

In one particular incident we filled the tray with water and bubbles and, using a straw, blew into the water and made more bubbles. One little boy in the group refused to give any eye contact at all. On my blowing the bubbles in the water, the young man looked fixedly at the bubbles and then at me. Then when given the straw he blew through it and made lots of bubbles. Now this may not sound such a great achievement, but his mum said afterwards that it was the first time that he had ever blown anything!

Straws and varying media are excellent means of encouraging motor movements in the mouth. For some children dribbling can be difficult to control. Speech therapists can suggest a variety of specialist activities, but I have found that straws can be really helpful. Children can be encouraged to blow into paint and washing-up liquid, and then, as they blow, the bubbly paint comes out of the container and prints can be taken. As an alternative to using paint, blowing bubbles in milkshake can be good fun, as can blowing the milkshake along a piece of paper.

Even the children with the most complex difficulties can engage in this sort of play. When I was teaching, we used some polystyrene chips from packaging and would plunge the children's feet into these. The warmth and the texture of the chips often encouraged feet movements and some leg movements.

Different textures of materials can also be used to encourage some gross motor movements. Corrugated paper sheets, bubble wrap, sheepskin mats and sandpaper can all be used to encourage standing, weight bearing and, for some children, just a greater awareness that their feet are on the ground.

For children with more complex difficulties, to encourage movement of feet, toes and legs, feet can be placed in large bowls of water, sand, flour, sterilized compost, rice, pasta, lentils. The children's feet can be moved passively in the bowls and observed to note any self-motivated movements.

For more physically able children, group activities around a large water tray filled with differing substances can also encourage balance and weight bearing when standing around the tub. The children can also be encouraged to explore with their hands and also to take part in pouring and scooping activities. This can move on to two-handed activities, for example holding a container with one hand and pouring something into it using the other hand. Another example is that of soap flakes mixed into water, and then bubbles created using a two-handed whisk. Again this requires the use of two hands. A new substance which has recently been introduced is 'Gellibaff', a mixture that when placed in water changes immediately to look and feel like jelly. This could be used in a bowl on a desk or table to encourage hand movements or placed in a bowl on the floor to encourage feet movements.

Another activity that could be used is aromatherapy. A foot spa can be purchased relatively inexpensively. It can be filled with either warm or cold water. The bottom of the foot spa is textured and when turned on gently massages the foot. It can be set to gentle or firm, and almost always will stimulate movements in the feet and will also encourage improved blood flow in the legs. Fragrant oils added to the water will calm or stimulate. Peppermint foot lotion can also be used on the feet and hands to help relax muscles.

Messy play can be used to encourage and stimulate both gross motor and fine motor development. We have used play dough for squeezing and opening and closing hands and for developing the use of the pointing finger. Big quantities of messy substances can also be good for helping fine motor skills. For example, make a large quantity of jelly in a single container, mix in some small objects and leave the jelly to set. The children can now push their hands into the jelly to find and pull out the objects. This could encourage the use of whole hand grasp and pincer grip and also passing objects from hand to hand. This activity could also be carried out with other substances, but it would need to be quite thick and deep.

Tinned tomatoes are another medium that can be used. The big plum tomatoes are especially useful. They are big enough to explode as they are squeezed, and this produces a wonderful sensory experience. The chopped tomatoes are also excellent for encouraging pincer grip and for poking and pointing skills.

In the encouragement of writing skills, messy play is also very useful. Often when starting to make marks a child will be given crayons or thick markers or chalks because they make marks easily and do not require much pressure. However, before giving a child any of these try some messy play to build up the basic skills.

Flour is a good substance to use. When it is placed on a black baking tray, patterns and marks are easily made and can be erased as the flour is smoothed over. Thus it can also be used again and again to practise the skills or movements – there is no need for lots of paper. However, there is lots of success because the marks made in the flour are easy to see against the background of the black tray.

When making circular marks a black polystyrene circular tray such as the ones a pizza is presented upon can be an excellent tool. The child can use the round shape of the tray as a prompt for the round movements. Once you have used flour you can then move on to cornflour and water, coloured rice, lentils, spaghetti and paint and squirty cream, and also thick icing sugar and water. All of this can be carried out individually or in a group setting.

Perspex is also good material to use because it is clear and the marks made in the various media can easily be seen from both sides. It is also very easy to clean and to keep germ free. Perspex is an excellent choice for children with more complex physical impairments who can be placed underneath to get a clear view of the movements made in the media. This can help to encourage eye contact, tracking and scanning.

A large piece of polythene (available from camping shops) or a cheap shower curtain laid out on the floor can also be used to provide the basis of some fun messy play. Sit the children around the polythene in a group. Onto the polythene sheet could be placed quantities of varying media which can be spread around with hands or feet, but not with the children standing because this would not be safe. Some wonderful marks can be made and this is good for encouraging some large gross motor movements. You could also use some coloured water, perhaps with some soap powder mixed in to thicken it, or thin sugar water with food colouring, or squirty cream sprayed onto the surface.

Space blankets could also be used for this. Again as a group the children could be seated around the blanket. They are great for squeezing and shaking and lifting up. These movements could be encouraged by placing different substances on the blanket such as leaves, cornflakes, pasta (either cooked or uncooked) or lentils, all of which make lovely sounds as well.

We have reached the end of this chapter looking at how messy play can assist the development of motor skills, and I hope once again that I have left you with food for thought and plenty of ideas to inspire you in your work. It should be remembered that these ideas are not designed to work in isolation but should be used as part of an overall strategy to encourage the development of motor skills.

8 RELAXATION

We all need to relax. Being able to relax is a skill that even adults do not learn very easily. We are all too busy rushing from place to place and doing so many activities and often do not take the time to truly relax. It is vital that children relax as well.

Even with children with special needs there is so much busyness in their lives. So many appointments to attend, so many groups to participate in, stays in hospital and even portage home visits to fit in. Some of the children also experience muscular spasms that can be quite painful, which can increase as more activity occurs. Being able to help a child to relax might ease such a spasm and then help the child to continue in another activity successfully where he would not otherwise be able or inclined to do so.

MESSY PLAY FOR RELAXATION

We all know that feeling that occurs after a long, busy day at work. Feeling tired and tense after a full day, probably arriving home with a stiff neck and sore eyes from an extensive period staring at the computer and wound up from a journey home stuck in traffic for an hour. On arrival you decide to run a hot bath and finally you step into it. It's the 'Aaah!' feeling that occurs as your tired body touches the warm water and the way the water seems to wrap itself around you and all the aches and pains and worries of the day just seem to melt away. In the same way that the bath helps you to relax, messy play can help children to relax.

Let me explain this with an example. I run a small lunchtime group on a Wednesday. The children arrive excited and hot and ready to play. We always begin with a story and then have lunch. It can be very difficult to read a story to children who are running around the room. Well, I hear you say, why don't you tell the story at another time? Well, in my example, that is not possible since the whole group is focused around the story. However, after the story the children have a choice between a table activity and messy play.

On one occasion the children had two bowls of porridge which we placed on the floor. The children continued to run around the room and then gradually one by one they approached the bowls. Little by little each child came and stood around the bowls. They reached in and stirred the porridge with their fingers and then went away. At first each one refused to touch the wet porridge. Then gradually each child stopped running and came and sat down by the bowls.

The child who had been the most active looked into the bowl, reached in and touched the porridge. He stirred it with the spoons, he scooped it and squeezed it with his hands. He sat with the porridge for at least ten minutes and did not want to stop when we had to draw the session to a close. His mum remarked that it was the calmest she had seen him and the most relaxed.

Early on in my teaching career I read some information that stated that the sound of a heartbeat is extremely relaxing for all people. I decided to use this information in creating a relaxing messy play environment for the children with whom I worked, based around the theme of the womb.

We had a small area that was called a solarium. It contained a very small almost hipbath pool in a room which looked like a very small swimming pool. It was very clinical, and whenever the children came into it they took a long time to relax and almost stiffened up. We looked around the room to see if there was anything we could change that would make the experience calmer and more relaxing.

The first thing we found was that it echoed considerably and could be very noisy and quite distracting. It was also very bright and the light reflected off the water. To alter some of these factors, we decided to try to change the environment.

The first thing we did was to cover all the windows with red and orange tissue paper. Then we placed orange food colouring in the water and added some gentle bubbles. We placed soft mats and towels on the floor and played a tape recording of a slow heartbeat. We found that in this environment the children were more able to become calm and relaxed. We also poured water gently over their feet to encourage this response. As the children improved week by week we also began to use some peppermint foot lotion and massaged it into their hands. The parents commented that when the children came home from school on those afternoons they were very calm and relaxed.

However, I should say that there were some members of staff who were very concerned by my methods and who warned me that if the heartbeat I used matched any of the children's then when I switched it off that child could have a heart attack and die. This really worried me and I stopped the activity immediately. Later when I was older and wiser I consulted with doctors who assured me that this reaction was absolutely impossible. Perhaps the lesson here is to check everything before you try it to ensure that it is safe in all aspects of its usage.

Some tips for relaxing messy play

If the child is allowed to explore at his own pace, on his own terms and no demands are being made on him to force the pace, playing with mess does become a relaxing experience. It is something that can be looked forward to, and once the children have experienced it and find that there is nothing to be scared of or worried about, the next time the large tub is brought out the children gather round with anticipation to see what you have brought along.

If you are wishing to create a relaxing experience then make sure you use calm, low-level voice tones. You must try not to become over-excited yourself, for your voice tone will set the tone of the session. It is always helpful to have some relaxing music playing in the background and this helps to set the tone of the activity. The children are always less likely to run around if the whole atmosphere is one of calm.

Make sure the movements you make in the media are slow and measured. Gradually move your hands around and around. Pour slowly and carefully and speak slowly and evenly as you talk about what you are doing.

Activities to aid relaxation:

- Pour lentils slowly over hands – it feels like water and is a slow steady movement.

- Pour warm water over hands.

- Pour rice slowly over hands.

- Move hands slowly around and round in smooth media such as custard, Angel Delight, condensed milk, evaporated milk.

- Move hands slowly around and around in rice, lentils and flour.

All of these activities can be carried out in a group or individual setting. Perhaps it would be a good idea for you to spend some time exploring the activities for yourself before you try them with the children with whom you work. Then not only would you be able to appreciate how the child might feel, you would also be able to anticipate responses and be able to channel them more positively.

Massage

It was important that you learn how to use massage products with children safely.

When I was teaching, we only ever massaged the children's hands and sometimes their feet. Now it is possible to learn about massage techniques through the baby massage courses that are run by most Sure Start areas. As a professional, I would suggest that massage be used only with the hands and feet. When families are undertaking this activity with their own children, they will have more flexibility and greater freedom to explore possibilities. To encourage this, it would be good to signpost families to the above courses to enable them to learn the appropriate skills and use them with their own children.

Hand and foot massage is a wonderful way of helping children relax and can also help hands which are quite stiff to become more supple as a preparation for working with those hands later on. There are a wide variety of wonderful smelling lotions and bubble baths which can be obtained from various shops, one of which is the Body Shop. I have found their products to be very gentle and excellent for quite sensitive skins. You could try other products found in most high street stores but it would be essential to check for allergic reactions, and the best guideline is to choose products with 'dermatologically tested' on the label.

Foot spas are also excellent for helping relaxation. They keep the water warm and their massaging levels can be set to be very gentle. However, you have to make sure that the spa is cleaned thoroughly after each use.

Vegetable oils are the best oils to use for hand massage. Baby oil can cause some friction and can be quite uncomfortable. Vegetable oils spread very easily and are very easy to add smelling oils to, but again you need to check first for allergic reactions and if you do not know then just use plain vegetable oil.

Eczema

Unfortunately a lot of children suffer from atopic eczema, and for these children it would not be advisable to use scents in their oils or in the water. It might be helpful to have a jar of aqueous cream to use with them instead. Aqueous cream also has the benefit that it can be added to water and can also be used in the foot spa.

Part Three

PRACTICAL MESSY PLAY IDEAS

9   DRY PLAY

Getting Started

For many people in my age group, children of the sixties, childhood should have been a time of freedom. However, not all of us had parents who were part of this ethos. Many of us, like me, had parents who had been brought up at the end of the war years and for them, the concept of wasting food was very much frowned upon. Not for us were the joys of exploring food with our fingers and tasting. No, for us it was 'Sit up straight, don't play with your food and remember there are people in the world who are far worse off than you.' I cannot walk down the street eating a chocolate bar without hearing my mother telling me to drop it or put it away.

I found the whole idea of playing with food very difficult until I had children of my own. I suddenly realized then that I did not want them to miss out on a whole range of experiences as I had done. Although I had engaged in messy play when I had been a teacher before having my own children, it really came into its own when I became a parent. Therefore I can understand when families are worried about messy play.

I never start with wet messy play although it is the most fun and offers the broadest range of experiences. I always start with dry messy play because it is less daunting and is easier to use with children who find it difficult to explore things with their hands. It is also a good means of introducing the whole idea of messy play to families and groups, because it is easily cleared away with a dustpan and brush. Here are some ideas for dry messy play.

DRY PLAY IDEAS
Cereals

Any cereals can be used so you don't have to go for the expensive ones; shops' own brand or value label is fine. I tend to use cornflakes, rice krispies, or porridge. They can be used for:

- plunging – cereals can be placed in large bowls and the child's feet plunged into them; the texture is very nice and it makes a good crunching sound

- squeezing, opening and closing hands

- scooping activities – beginning with hands, large scoops, big spoons and then small spoons

- controlled pouring activities – water is quite an uncontrollable medium so dry ingredients are easier and less messy; pouring them over the back of closed hands gives a relaxing feeling and can also encourage the hands to open.

Rice

Rice is also lovely to use it has a wonderful flowing property and can feel like water in its movement. However, it is rather a bland colour. You can add colour yourself and make it really exciting. Place the rice in a bowl and add a few drops of food colouring. Mix the rice and colouring until all the rice is coloured. Then place the rice on a baking sheet and place in a very cool oven for a minute or two until it is all completely dry. Wait for the rice to cool down before using.

Rice can be placed in a large container and used in a group activity. It can be poured, explored with hands, scooped into containers. The rice can be scooped in turns. An extension of this activity would be to provide clear empty bottles to be placed in the rice. The children can then use the bottles for putting the rice into either by hand or with a spoon, or the bottles can be pushed along in the rice so that the rice fills the bottles. Lids can then be placed on the bottles and they can be used as musical instruments. This adds a good auditory dimension to the overall experience.

As an individual activity rice can be placed in a tray in front of the child and poured, scooped and explored. If the adult sits in front of the child it is a wonderful opportunity for good eye contact. The rice can also be used with normal water toys such as paddle funnels because it flows like water.

Lentils

There are many sorts of lentils, of all colours and sizes – yellow split peas, green split peas, continental lentils, red split lentils – they are all great to play with and explore.

Yellow split peas are great for plunging your hands into and exploring. They feel wonderful, with the same flowing property of water and they feel cool. Placed in a small but deep container they are great for hiding stretchy animals in. I used this with a boy who was gastro fed. His mum and dad had great difficulties in keeping him seated during the feeding, since he had learnt to walk and to get down from a chair. His parents decided to give him a tray full of yellow lentils and stretchy animals, which he loved to explore with his hands, and they found that this activity maintained his interest, kept up his concentration and kept him seated during the 20-minute feed. They also gained a lot of eye contact and he was incredibly happy.

A lot of my families do not like the red lentils at first because they do behave rather like water. When poured out of the container or dropped on the floor they spread everywhere and they can be rather tedious to clear up after the session. However, unlike water they do not soak into carpets. They do feel very nice when poured over hands or feet and they can be easily swept up with a dustpan and brush.

To give a wider range of experiences, all types of lentils can be placed in bowls and litter trays and children can have their feet placed into them. The lentils can then be poured over the feet and this can encourage little movements in the feet and toes and even kicking movements, which of course is great fun!

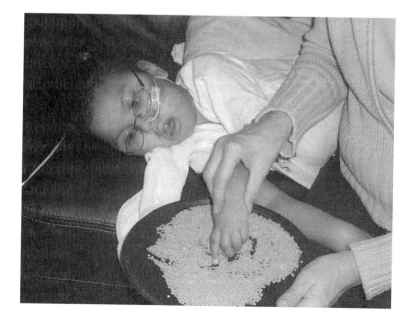

Flour

This can be any kind of flour and one should always take into account food intolerance and allergies. However, it does not need to be the supermarket's finest brand because it is not going to be eaten or used for cooking. The cheapest bag of flour is probably the best to use; it does not matter if it is plain or self-raising – it just needs to be flour.

- Flour is very fine, soft and smooth. Clapping your hands in it produces interesting results… clouds of flour can be very exciting. Please be careful with flour as it would not be helpful if the child were to inhale large amounts of it, especially if she already experiences difficulties with breathing.

- Flour can be grasped, lifted and dropped, and makes a nice plopping sound when dropped in a large bowl of flour.

- It can be poured through a water paddle and a sieve and can look like snow and feel interesting if you place your hands underneath and try to catch it.

- You can use it like sand and pack it into bowls and buckets, turn it over and create flour castles, which of course can be immediately pounded down, which is very exciting!

- You can add powder paint in different colours to the flour and turn it into coloured flour. The bright colours can be used to encourage attention and concentration skills. Red, yellow, orange are the best colours to use.

- Glitter can also be added to the flour to make it sparkle.

- If you have access to a UV room then playing with flour in here can be very effective for eye contact and attention skills.

- You can add spices, milkshake powder, chocolate powder to the flour to add to an olfactory sensory experience.

Pasta

Pasta is wonderful stuff. It comes in so many shapes and sizes and, these days, different colours.

- Tortiglioni and rigatoni are expensive pastas, but apart from cannelloni they have the largest holes in a tube and so can be used very successfully to develop threading skills before moving on to using beads.

- Pasta can be coloured rather like rice and if you used fluorescent paint, again this could be used very successfully in a UV room.

- Long spaghetti can be used for a two-handed activity, for example snapping the spaghetti in two. This can also be used as an activity to strengthen hands and to encourage grasping.

- Ribbon or bow pasta is great for crunching with hands or standing on to crunch, which encourages stepping, and of course it makes a great sound, which continues to encourage movement.

- Spiral or fusilli pastas feel very nice, as does macaroni and penne.

- Lasagne is great for snapping and crunching.

- Of course, like rice, pasta can be placed in a bottle or a container and can create a lovely sound.

- It can be placed in a large bowl and can be explored with the hands and feet.

- It can be scooped with hands, spoons and spades and passed from one bowl to another and from hand to hand.

- It can also be used for very controlled pouring activities.

Polystyrene chips or maize chips

You have to be very careful with polystyrene chips, and they really do carry a warning with them. If you use them with a child *you must must must make sure that you keep a close watch on the child to ensure that he does not put any in his mouth.* This is because polystyrene chips expand in water and, if swallowed, would expand in the child's stomach.

These chips are best used in a large cardboard box with the child sitting and then plunging his feet into the chips. They feel warm and they make a soft crunchy noise when trodden on. I used these when teaching in London in what was then called a 'special care' unit. The children in my class had very limited movement and also had additional sensory difficulties. The children sat in Tumbleform chairs. We took off their shoes and socks and poured the polystyrene chips all over the floor onto their feet. They loved it and it created lots of squeals of delight and some very excited feet movements.

The chips could also be used for plunging hands in and encouraging opening and closing movements. Or they can be poured and dropped from a height to encourage tracking, eye contact and attention skills.

Shredded paper

If you live in a local authority area like mine then you will find that shredded paper cannot be recycled because it is too small to go through the paper sorting grader at the recycling plant. So, in many parts of England we are putting into our non-recyclable bins something that can be used again.

Shredded paper is great for exploring with hands and feet. In fact if you have enough it can be spread all over the floor and used to encourage rolling, crawling and standing. It feels different to ordinary paper, and makes a satisfying crunching sound as it is moved on.

- It is strong enough to be pulled.

- It can be used to make piles encouraging use and understanding of concepts such as on, on top, etc., and then can be pushed down.

- It can also be used to encourage small hand movements like tearing and to develop scissor skills like snipping.

- Placed on top of a shiny survival blanket it can increase the tactile stimulation of a child, and auditory stimulation is enhanced because there are two sounds produced by the activity, the rustling of the paper and the crackling sound of the survival blanket.

- Again in a UV room the shredded paper would produce some exciting experiences.

If your shredder is a cross-cutting shredder, the paper will be almost in a confetti state. This offers a range of new and different experiences.

- This would again be good to use in controlled pouring activities in a large container.

- If you collected enough, it would also be good to use in a large container on the floor for feet and hand plunging to encourage feet and hand movement.

- In smaller quantities, it would be good for spooning into a small container or for filling various sized containers.

- It might be used to encourage some precise pincer grip movements.

- You could try dropping from a height to encourage eye contact and attention skills.

Buttons

I know when I was a little girl there was nothing that I liked better on a rainy afternoon than being allowed to explore my Nan's button box. They were in a large tin that was embossed on the outside with an array of beautifully coloured animals, which felt so nice as you moved your fingers over them. The buttons sounded noisy in the tin, and if I tipped the tin in different ways the sound changed, and that was very exciting. On opening the tin there were a variety of pleasant smells that accosted my nose, because the buttons were all made of different materials. There were many different colours and shapes and sizes to explore. However, what I loved to do most of all was push my hands in amongst them and feel their coldness and the way they moved over my hands like water. It was always a very pleasant afternoon spent with the button box.

It is this experience that I would like other children to encounter. I have spoken to lots of adults, and button boxes are something that many of us played with in our childhood and something that we remember with pleasure.

Buttons can be quite expensive these days, especially as they have become quite specialized and can be considered a fashion statement. Now I do not want to make a fashion statement and I do not really mind what the buttons look like. Therefore you might want to ask friends or colleagues for any old buttons they might have in order to get your own button box off to a good and inexpensive start. If you are throwing away a piece of clothing, make sure you cut off the buttons. Visit your local charity shops – sometimes they have boxes of buttons that can be bought quite cheaply. Or you could just be very lucky like me and live near to a factory that makes buttons and sometimes when they have runs where the colour has failed or been streaky they might be quite happy to give you their discarded ones for a small price.

Buttons are great for all the reasons I stated previously. They can be:

- poured
- picked up with a pincer grip
- scooped
- plunged into
- transferred from hand to hand
- threaded
- posted
- stacked
- put into a container to shake and make music with.

A variety could also be sewn onto a piece of material to provide a new tactile experience.

Snow

Now I know as you read this you are thinking: 'What is she talking about? Snow is wet, it melts and you can only get it at certain times of the year – if you are lucky!' Yes that is all correct, but I am talking about fake snow. If you remember the wonderful film *The Lion, the Witch and the Wardrobe*, you will recall that snow plays a large part in the story. The film was shot and produced in New Zealand, but there was not enough snow and so they had to use fake snow. The snow they used really did look like real snow and the actors and actresses said that it felt like it too.

Well, I have found some fake snow called Insta Snow. It costs around £5 for a small tub. In the tub are some granules that become snow when a little water is added. In fact the whole tub, which you can hold in your hand, can make five gallons of snow! It is quite amazing! It is incredible to watch it turn into snow.

This is actually something that you can do with the children. You place two small scoops into a bowl and add a small amount of water and the granules and water just expand immediately 'as if by magic'! It changes from small hard white granules to soft fluffy snow in seconds! However, what is most remarkable is that when you put your hand into the snow it feels cold and wet, yet when you remove your hand it is dry!

As you can imagine this is a wonderful sensory experience for the children. Something is dry yet it feels wet, and it is also cold. It is also very white and so as I have said before, if used in a room with UV lighting, it will also encourage good looking and tracking skills.

The fake snow can be grasped and will help with strengthening hands and grasping skills. It can also be poured into containers and poured over hands to encourage opening and closing.

Moonsand

This is a relatively new product that I discovered last year. Actually it was one of my families that discovered it. As far as I know it is only available in Argos. It comes in a large pack with scoops, trowels and shapes, and a handy carry case. It is also available in a smaller pack of six containers with different coloured sand in them.

What is remarkable about this sand is that it can be moulded just like ordinary sand but it does not need water to be added to it to make it hold its shape. When it falls on the floor it can be picked up easily in the same way that you use Blu-tack to pick up Blu-tack. Once again it is messy, but because it is still dry it can be easily cleared up, which for many people really is a bonus.

The little girl who used this sand has spinal muscular atrophy (SMA) Type 1 and finds movements very difficult. She also finds picking up and moving or holding or indeed lifting anything heavy – even the slightest bit heavy – extremely troublesome. However, she and her parents have found that this sand can be picked up and grasped with the slightest movement and is light enough to be easily scooped. For her it is an excellent medium.

As with all other dry ingredients Moonsand has many uses. It can be:

- squeezed
- grasped
- moulded
- scooped

- poured (in its loose state)
- explored with the hands and feet, because unlike normal sand it does not stick.

The only thing with this sand is that unlike normal sand you must not add water to it. It will completely upset the sand's properties. However, in its moulded state it can be floated on water and then dried before replacing in its tub.

Sawdust

Sawdust is yet another dry medium that can be used in messy play. However, it again is something that carries a health warning and you have to be quite careful using. Sawdust comes in all grades, and you cannot use the sawdust from the garden when you have been sawing a piece of wood! The sawdust used for dry messy play has to be clean, sterile and of quite a fine grade, probably the sort of sawdust that is used as bedding for a small pet like a a hamster. The finely graded sawdust is soft and smooth, and it is safe. Some sawdust of a bigger grade may be cheaper but it often has shards of wood in it that can be quite dangerous.

Sawdust can be used in a small bowl for one-to-one work, or in a large bowl for some group work. There can be a lot of turn taking and playing and chatting around the container. This is again a medium that can have some quite messy results especially if the children become overexcited and start to throw it around. Therefore, as always, it is good to have a large broom and a dustpan and brush to clean up the mess.

Sawdust can be:

- scooped
- poured
- made into piles
- grasped
- transferred from hand to hand

- explored with hands and feet in large containers
- poured from a height to encourage concentration and attention.

Sand

Sand is always the medium which people naturally think will be used for messy play. It has been used for many years and it still has its uses. It is not my favourite medium for reasons I will share below. However, when beginning messy play with a family or child, it is a familiar concept and therefore not so threatening as some of the other media I like to use, and so it is generally received less warily.

In its dry state sand feels velvety smooth. The best type to use is the play sand widely available in all good toyshops. I would not recommend the use of building sand or sharp sand. Although these are cheaper, they are of a rougher texture and can stain the skin with a yellow colour, which can take considerable effort with soap and water to remove.

As with flour, coloured powder paint and glitter can be added to the sand to increase the visual sensory experience. Sand can be used for:

- pouring
- scooping
- grasping
- transferring from hand to hand
- catching when dropped from a height
- exploring with hands and feet in a large container
- placing into containers.

The only difficulty with sand is that as everyone knows you must be careful not to get it in the child's eyes or between toes because the grainy feeling can make skin very sore if the sand is not removed completely at the end of the messy play session.

Other media

Many other ingredients can be used, either in a one-to-one or a group situation, and can be used for scooping, pouring, grasping and exploring with hands and feet. Some can also be placed under certain surfaces and when walked upon make a lovely crunching sound.

- crushed digestive biscuits
- skimmed milk powder
- icing sugar
- milkshake powder
- talcum powder
- bath salts
- bath confetti
- compost
- dried leaves (washed and dried in an oven on a low heat)
- other dried pulses
- bulghur wheat
- cous-cous
- soap flakes
- tapioca (this feels like the polystyrene chips inside bean bags and flows like water)
- cocoa powder
- dry porridge
- popped popcorn
- cotton wool in balls and in a strip (although if you are like me it can put your teeth on edge as it shreds)
- gravy granules
- breadcrumbs – fresh and toasted.

This is by no means an exhaustive list, but I do hope it gives you some ideas to try and will spur you on to explore other media.

So now you have all the ideas. Why not go ahead and try some play with some of these ingredients? It probably is best to start with something that is the least threatening, and I would suppose that with this in mind shredded paper is the best place to start. Once you have begun with this you can move on to something a little more adventurous but less familiar, perhaps lentils and pasta. However, once you have started you will find that it is not easy to stop, one success will lead naturally to another. So, it's over to you now – dive in and try!

10 WET PLAY

MOVING ON TO WET MESSY PLAY

Wet play really does produce many different responses in different people. Wet is something that we Britons are accustomed to, after all there is always precipitation of one form or another in our 'green and pleasant land'. However, although we are familiar with it, that does not mean that we actually enjoy being wet or the mess that is associated with it. Therefore, this is the hurdle that you have to get over when working with children and families.

Some children do not mind exploring dry media but wet media can create a very different and negative response. They can withdraw hands and become quite upset. In order to overcome this sort of reaction you need to think carefully about experiences that might bridge the gap. I feel that the way to encourage engagement with wet play is to continue to use dry play but then move through a series of experiences that move the child on to an acceptance of wet play and the experiences it offers.

First, alter the texture of, say, sand so that the substance becomes quite lumpy. Having done this then move to something non-threatening like lentils, which pour like water and feel like water. Once this is accepted move on to fake snow (see chapter 9), which is dry but feels wet, then water on its own, and then gradually increase the range of wet textures used. It is always important to introduce new experiences slowly and to go at the child's pace, to make it fun and never force the child to do anything he really does not want to.

As a professional working with families or groups, you must remember that it is not your home or building and you need to be respectful. You need to gain trust that you will always bring things that can be easily cleaned away and do not leave stains. As with the child, you will need to go at the family's and group's pace and never force any experience. You gain nothing by doing this.

There are many things that can be used for wet messy play, and the majority of these things can be found in your kitchen cupboard, so they do not have to be expensive. You won't be using any of the food media for cooking, so they do not have to be premium-grade ingredients. They are only going to be used for exploring and so can be from the basic range at your local supermarket, which will help to keep costs low. It is amazing how so many ordinary materials can be used in so many differing ways to achieve a wide range of experiences for the child. Here are some of the ones which I have found to be most useful.

Water

Water is and has always been a major component in messy play. It can be liquid or solid, warm or cool, and all variations can be great fun and very rewarding.

- It can be used as a relaxant – pouring warm water over a tightly clasped hand can help the hand to open. It can also be used to encourage pouring and splashing.

- It can be used as a solid as ice. Yes, it is very cold, but crushed it can quickly begin to melt and this can be a lovely experience. The pieces of ice could also be used to encourage a pincer grip or they could also be used to squeeze and encourage some whole hand grasp or for strengthening a weak muscular hand movement.

- Water can be coloured using food colouring, and this can be lots of fun for pouring.

Bubble baths can be added to the water and lots of bubbles created. These can be used to bring hands together and clap the bubbles, and the bubbles can be popped to encourage the use of the pointing index finger. Big handfuls of bubbles can also be squeezed. The smell of the bubble baths can also stimulate the olfactory centres, which can relax or stimulate depending on the smells used. A little note of caution, though: some children – especially those with skin conditions such as eczema – can be allergic to specific chemicals within certain bubble baths, so check with the parents or carers in advance.

Jelly

Jelly is wonderful. It has a strong smell and a wonderful colour, both of which are very stimulating to the senses, but it also has a wonderful texture, which can change from solid to semi-solid and then to liquid as it is explored. It is also very cold when chilled to its solid form. Jelly can be used in all its states.

- As a solid it can be used to develop hand strength through lots of squeezing, and to encourage opening and closing of hands and pointing. It is a wonderful medium to poke a finger into, and it makes a lovely slurpy sound as you do this.

- You can melt the jelly and then place objects in it. Once this is placed in the fridge and set this can be used for finding an object, getting it out and putting it back in. If the objects are small enough then a pincer grip can be encouraged to remove the objects.

- It can be used for scooping, where with hands or a small spoon the jelly can be scooped into a small container – very messy but great fun!

- If the jelly is chopped up into squares it can be used for squeezing, and for practising pincer grip by picking up the chopped pieces out of a bowl or from a tray.

- Again in its chopped state, jelly can also be used to encourage bringing hands together and clapping.

- As a liquid it can be used for pouring and for encouraging opening and closing of hands if it is poured over a hand.

- It can be used for placing since when the object is placed in melted jelly a small splash occurs which encourages more placing.

- Finally, it can be used for just exploring and having fun.

Tinned tomatoes

These are my favourites, but I know they are not to everyone's taste. However, like jelly they are so incredibly versatile!

- Plum tomatoes are great for squeezing and encouraging opening and closing of hands. They feel very slimy, they smell tomatoey and when squeezed they make that satisfying gloop pop, and the children just love it!

- The shape of plum tomatoes makes them great for poking, pointing and encouraging use of one finger.

- Chopped tomatoes can also be very nice to explore. They can be patted, poked and pushed around. They move very smoothly and as they move they make a satisfying slurping sound.

- They can also be used to encourage a pincer grip, as the chopped pieces are small enough to be picked up this way.

- Finally, chopped tomatoes can be scooped into small containers and used to encourage using the hands together.

Baked beans

Many people really hate baked beans and when cold they do not smell at all appetizing and can make some people feel quite nauseous. This then is one medium that has to be used with caution as far as the adults are concerned, although generally the children do not mind.

- The smell of baked beans is very stimulating (for the children at least!) and you will often find the children will lick their lips when they smell them.

- They are great for scooping, pouring and squeezing. Again they are a wonderful tactile experience.

- The beans can be used to encourage a pincer grip.

- Like the tomatoes they have a wonderful sensory movement which is pleasing to watch as they are pushed around and so they can help concentration and observation.

Rice pudding

Rice pudding is very like baked beans in the reactions it can produce – you either love it or you hate it! This again is something that you have to be very aware of when planning the session. I worked with a young lady who was profoundly multiply handicapped, but the thing that provoked the most response from her was messy play. We had successfully used condensed milk and it was a medium she thoroughly enjoyed exploring and would squeeze and slap and clap her hands.

Having had so much success with this, I decided it was time to extend the experience and move on to rice pudding. However, she was having none of it! She immediately pulled a face when the tin was opened and turned her whole upper body away when cold rice pudding was placed in front of her. Her mum wanted to continue to see if she would accept the medium. Her mum tried to place her hands into it but again the young lady pulled away, and this time became quite upset. We decided not to force the issue any more on that day, but tried again the following week. However, her response

was the same. It was interesting that when she later tried eating rice pudding as part of her solid food introduction she really did not like it. So in this case No! really did mean No!

- Cold rice pudding has a thick consistency with little lumps in it. This gives it a great tactile value and can be used with either feet or hands to provide a wide range of sensory activities.

- It also has a very sweet smell and is very sticky when drying, again adding to the sensory experience.

- It can be used for pouring, scooping and picking up using a pincer grip.

Cooked spaghetti

Cooked spaghetti has a life of its own and is wonderful for exploring in messy play! After cooking, you will need to wash it in cold water to cool it down and remove the starch, and then drain it. Once this has been done, the spaghetti will move very smoothly over a surface. It is very easy to push around with even the smallest movements of the hands or feet (a small addition of vegetable oil will also assist the movement).

You can then add liquid paint to the spaghetti, which adds a new colour, or possibly many colours, to the experience. The coloured spaghetti can be pushed around and around the surface creating some very interesting patterns and of course a lot of mess. It is a wonderful sensory experience. This helps concentration and observation. You could always lay a piece of sugar paper onto the painty spaghetti and take a print, which will create some interesting art to take home. And try doing this with a piece of perspex to create a close-up visual delight!

Condensed milk

Here I mean *condensed* milk, not evaporated milk. It is a lot thicker and stickier. It is quite expensive but worth considering because it has so many uses.

- It is great for squeezing, scooping and exploring.
- It is excellent for encouraging two-handed play. Place both hands in and move them around and then bring hands

together and clap. It is very sticky, feels lovely and also makes a lovely sound as hands are clapped together.

- As it is on your hands it has a very sweet smell, which is very pleasant and usually encourages hand-to-mouth exploration and some good observation.

Evaporated milk

This also has its place in the world of messy play. It is quite thin in consistency compared with condensed milk (described above) but not as thin as ordinary milk. It also has a different smell.

- It is great for exploring with hands or fingers
- It can be used to encourage pouring as hand-eye skills become more controlled.

Angel Delight

I know this is very sweet and contains an incredible amount of sugar, but in my work I do not use this for eating. It is purely for play and tactile experiences. It comes in a great variety of bright colours, which together with a very strong smell encourage observation.

- It can be made thick or thin. When thick it is great for plunging or squeezing and feels very nice as it pours through your fingers.
- In a very thin state it can be used for pouring and scooping.
- In its semi-solid state it can be great to hide things in and then for putting in and taking out objects.
- It is also good for exploring with hands and feet.

Golden syrup

This is truly wonderful stuff! It has a lovely colour, is very shiny and clear, and catches the light. It smells wonderful and it feels so nice. It is very sticky and offers a great tactile experience. It can be used in similar ways to condensed milk but it flows more slowly and so can be a bit of a surprise when tipping and pouring when it suddenly emerges in a great mass. It is fairly unpredictable, but great fun!

Banana

Bananas can be used whole or mashed or in slices.

- As whole bananas, they can be used for squeezing and strengthening hands.
- They can be cut into pieces and used to encourage pincer grips.
- In pieces, they are also good for encouraging finger feeding.
- They can be mashed and are then good for exploring with hands and feet.

You should check with the child's parents or carers before using banana flavour as some children may react negatively to it.

Milkshake powder

Milkshake powder is another of my favourite messy play substances. It comes in many flavours so offers a range of smells. It can be used dry or mixed with water so offers a range of tactile options. Dry, it has a gritty texture which is great for finger pointing, making marks in and for exploring with hands. When wet it is also interesting. You only want to add water to it, and just enough to make it a stiff mixture. Once mixed, it produces a strong smell and is still quite grainy yet smooth at the same time. Again, this gives a great sensory experience which is both tactile, olfactory and gustatory.

When wet it can also be used for a whole group activity. The mixture can be placed on or in a surface, the children can stand or sit around it and a group activity of pushing the mixture around the table can be arranged. This will be good for encouraging turn taking, eye contact and observation. The mixture is also so thick that a print can be taken of it by laying a large piece of sugar paper on top. As the sugar paper dries, it can be pinned or stuck on the wall and a wonderful smell will spread through the room. When it is fully dry, its texture leaves a rough surface (like mountains!) to explore with your hands.

There are lots of flavours of dry powder but the best are strawberry, banana and lime because of their vivid colours and strong smells... but check before you use the banana one as some children react negatively to the small of bananas.

Clean mud

There is a school of thought today that believes that children do not need to be exposed to germs and bugs as used to be the case. It would appear that all the things that used to make life fun when I was a child are now frowned upon and, in many cases, actively discouraged. As a child I loved just digging in the mud in the garden, and my sister had the peculiar habit of transporting mud from one end of the garden to another in the box at the back of her large tricycle. None of us know why she did this. But then does there always have to be a reason for doing something – can we not just want to have fun in a certain activity because we do, not because there is some grand psychological reason for it?

Playing in the mud is one experience that I feel children miss out on in our current society. For a start, many children do not have a garden in which to play, and then there are too many worries about the bugs that they might catch through touching the soil. In view of this, many may be unwilling to encourage children to play with earth or mud.

However, I do find that compost is a good alternative to this. When I mentioned this to my colleagues they were rather worried, thinking that I meant the compost I make in the composter in my garden from all my kitchen waste, grass cuttings, etc., and which is regularly frequented by the local wildlife. Of course not! What I mean is the sterile compost that you can buy from most garden centres. It does not have to be a special one – just a bag of ordinary, cheap compost.

- Compost can be used in a group situation very successfully. The whole bag can be poured into a large bowl or tray. The children can sit or stand around the bowl and explore it with their hands or feet. They can also use spoons and spades if desired.

- It is quite damp when it first comes out of the bag, but once opened it soon dries out. You will need to add some water in order to make mud. The children can mix the water in as it is added, which encourages hand grip, stirring and arm co-ordination.

- Once it has been turned into mud, there can be further exploring with hands and feet, squeezing, lifting and dropping this new substance.

Compost is fantastic to use and it is safe. It is also very messy! If you are going to use this indoors, I would recommend the use of a large plastic sheet to cover the floor, as the children do become very excited and animated with the compost and a lot of it can end up spread around the room. You need to be very relaxed about this and leave cleaning up until the end, otherwise it can be like 'shovelling snow while it is still snowing' as the well-known saying goes.

Shaving foam, crazy soap and aerosol cream

All three of these have a wonderful texture, very light and airy, and as they are touched the tiny bubbles pop and make a fizzing sound. When the hands are clapped together the foam will float into the air, which can be quite exciting for the child. However, with shaving foam and crazy soap you have to be careful because if rubbed in the eyes it can sting.

- All foams can be sprayed onto a shiny survival blanket. The blanket enables the foams to be moved around easily. It is a wonderful way of exploring using hands and feet. There is also the visual stimulus of the shiny blanket, and the added auditory stimulus of the blanket crinkling as the foam is moved across it.

- The foam can also be spread upon perspex and large mirrors. This is a very good visual experience because you can spray the foam onto the mirror and then scrape it off and the child can see himself underneath.

Mashed potato

You can of course use fresh potato, but I have found the best one to use is that found in packets, which requires less preparation time and you can make up as much or as little as you need for each session.

Mashed potato is again a good medium to use in a large bowl in a group setting. It can be mixed in the large container while the children are all there and the children can all stir and watch as the powder and water mix together and turn into mashed potato. They can do this with their hands and this would be a great experience, or they could use spoons and large spades.

- It could be coloured using food colouring and this would encourage some visual stimulation, as would coloured sugar strands and glitter.

- Objects could also be hidden in the mashed potato, which is good for encouraging searching through, putting in and taking out. If the objects are small enough then a pincer grip can be encouraged.

- If the mashed potato is quite thick and firm then it can be used for squeezing and scooping activities.

Porridge oats

This is a medium very much like mashed potato. Again it can be used to great effect when used in a group. When mixed with water, it gives quite a sticky, thick but grainy consistency.

- It is great for a tactile exploration session and is also good for scooping activities.

- It is also good for squeezing.

- It can also be used dry and the children can mix in the water using jugs to pour and spoons and spades to stir; again tactile experience can be enhanced by allowing the children to mix with their hands.

Ready-made custard

I have found this to be a great favourite with both parents and colleagues. Of course, it is already made up so there is less time and effort in preparation and none of that long laborious stirring and pulling in and out of the microwave to see if it is cooked.

- It is a lovely bright colour and it feels very smooth.

- It is a wonderful sensory tactile experience if it is poured through your fingers or explored with the hands. Custard is good for pouring, but will need to be watered down a little, otherwise it emerges in a big gloop.

- It has a very strong smell, which encourages hand-to-mouth exploration.

Custard, like milkshake, can also be used to produce 'works of art'. It can be coloured with food colouring. You can use any colour you like, but it is probably best to choose the brighter colours for maximum sensory stimulation. The custard can then be placed on a piece of smooth paper, not sugar paper this time because that might soak it up. The children can then push the custard around on the paper and make lots of interesting patterns. It can then be left to dry and hung on the wall.

Instant hot chocolate powder

This powder does not mix very easily with cold water. It has to be mixed with a little water to a paste first and then more water added.

However, you always end up with some powder floating on the mixture. This does not really matter as it just adds to the whole sensory experience, and can become a wet/dry experience.

- This is very good for exploring with hands and feet because the dry lumps can open out when squeezed.

- It has a very strong chocolatey smell, which increases the olfactory experience and will encourage some hand-to-mouth exploration

- It is lovely for pouring.

Sugar

Sugar comes in various forms, and the more grainy it is the more tactile the experience. However, in my experience, the best form of sugar to be used in the wet state is icing sugar.

Icing sugar can be mixed thickly as a paste, which can be spread about using fingers or hands to produce many mountainous creations. The paste can also be coloured to give a variation of colours and shades and achieve maximum visual effect. Or it can be used in a thin state for exploring with hands, clapping with and also for producing some lovely sticky feelings. In this state it could also be used for pouring.

In can also be watered down to a very thin mixture which is almost clear. This can be spread on a piece of paper with the hands and then pinches of powder paint can be dropped on it. This produces an immediate star effect, which happens right in front of your eyes and is a wonderful visual stimulant as the paints spread, as if by magic, across the page. When the picture is completed, the sugar and paint mixture dries with a shiny colourful glaze which is very eye catching.

Sand mousse

This was recommended to me by a colleague. To make this you need sand, washing-up liquid, a whisk and food colouring. You put the sand in a bowl and put some washing-up liquid into it. You will have to experiment with how much because it depends on how much sand you use. Then using the whisk, whisk fast for a few minutes, adding more washing-up liquid if necessary until it begins to look and feel like mousse. Once whisked add any colour that you wish. It can be stored in an airtight container. This is a very good tactile and visual experience.

REMEMBER!

All of these wet activities are extremely messy, and in a group situation the children can become rather exuberant and mess can be spread. Once one child begins to throw, then the rest of the group is sure to follow and much laughter and excitement will ensue. Now this can be great fun, but really this is not what we want to achieve from the sessions, although the social aspects of children having fun together cannot be denied. It also means that the mess can very quickly cover the children, their clothes, their hair and the other adults present. It is important to reassure the family that the mess can all be cleaned or washed away easily and will not stain.

However, the one substance which needs to be given special consideration is jelly. I found this out when using it in its liquid state with a boy I used to work with. He was having a great time splashing in the jelly, giving good eye contact and taking turns. When I had finished he needed a bath and I needed to go home and change my clothes, neither of which seemed to present any particular concerns. However, the next morning I discovered that I could not comb my hair because the wet jelly had set. If you use jelly and it gets in your hair you need to wash it out as soon as possible.

I am sure that in this chapter I have barely scraped the surface of the wonders of wet messy play. I am sure that there are more experiences to be discovered and that I shall venture into as time goes by. As I am sitting here writing, I am wondering about the use of gravy in its various states and flavours. It would also be possible to explore more of the tinned milky puddings such as tapioca, macaroni and semolina. All of these would have widely differing textures and pouring properties and would be wonderful to explore.

I hope that I have given you some food for thought and that you will try these and some of your own ideas when you next venture into wet messy play.

11 NON-MESSY PLAY

I know I can hear you saying, 'What is she talking about? This is a book about messy play but now you are talking about messy play with no mess?' How can you have messy play with no mess? Well, you can...

Some children and adults are tactile defensive. By this I mean that they do not want to engage directly with any medium with their hands or feet. The reasons for this may be a previous bad experience, or perhaps the adults in the child's life may not like mess and have transferred this concern to the child, or the child may have a particular problem with tactile sensations. In chapter 9 we discussed dry play as a medium for encouraging those who are worried about mess to explore and play safely. However, for some tactile defensive children and adults even beginning with dry mess is something that is too much of a challenge and cannot be considered. Therefore as parents or professionals we have to find another way of engaging them, and that way of engaging has to be safe and non-threatening for the children or adults concerned.

POINTS TO CONSIDER

Attitude

As parents or professionals we have to be flexible enough to change our own attitudes. It could be that we have experienced the child's negative response to media on previous occasions and so we come to any new experience with a certain amount of fear and concern. When this occurs it can be easy to transfer our own negative feelings to the child. When this happens the child may feel worried and respond negatively because she mirrors the fact that we are worried.

In order to help the child to move forward all those involved need to be positive, calm and controlled. It is probably best if the adults model the activity for the child and show that it is nothing to be afraid of. I think the best policy with children is that you should never try to encourage a child, or indeed anyone, to do something that you are not comfortable doing yourself.

Practice

Another idea which can help is to make sure that the person presenting the activity has tried it out for him- or herself before attempting to introduce it to the child. By exploring the media away from the child in your own time you can try it for yourself and note how it made you feel. Try to listen to your own responses and consider whether this would produce the same response in the child. What senses does it stimulate? Is it too strong or too weak? Use the information from your own experience to decide if it would be good to try this with the child.

Preparation

You have to remember at the end of the day that the best-laid plans of mice and men can always change, and sometimes very suddenly. In doing this kind of activity you do have to do a lot of preparation. You have to make sure that the particular activity chosen is one that can be carried out safely, is appropriate for the physical setting and the child's stage of development, and in which, as far as you know, the child will be happy to engage. However, even with thorough preparation, you have to recognize that, as with everything that you plan to do with children, you have to have a 'Plan B'or alternative activity that you can offer if things don't go well or something unexpected happens.

Individuality

Each person is an individual and reacts as an individual. An activity that you have carried out successfully with one child may not necessarily be so successful with another. Conversely, if unsuccessful with one child that does not mean that it can never be used again, because another child may react differently. No messy play activity is guaranteed to work well with all children all the time. You must consider the needs of the child, her stage of development and the desires of the parents and choose the activity accordingly. There are many non-messy play options to choose from.

IDEAS TO ENCOURAGE NON-MESSY PLAY

Wellington boots

Wellies are wonderful, and they are a real godsend to anyone engaging in messy play. Armed with our wellies on our feet the child and accompanying adults can have a lot of fun – even if they don't want to actually touch the messy substance!

You can walk through mud, splash in water, stomp through the sand and wander through paint without getting messy. And having walked through the various media you can step onto paper and look at all the wonderful footprints that you have made.

Gloves

What wellies are to feet, gloves can be to hands! Gloves can be used to encourage children to engage in mess with their hands without actually getting them messy at all. You can choose different thicknesses of gloves depending on how concerned the child is – thin gloves will avoid the need to touch the material but still allow the temperature of the media to be felt, thick gloves will remove the sensation of coldness. There are also tactile gloves, which are quite thick and which have different textures on them offering a range of tactile experiences.

Gloved hands and fingers can be used to explore all kinds of media to make handprints, fingerprints or other interesting patterns in the medium itself. Or they can be used to make prints on paper for later display.

You should also bear in mind that some children may find that having their hands enclosed within gloves is not a positive experience. If this happens, allowing them to place their hands on your hands may be less threatening. The child can then explore the media with you and can feel the movements of your hand but does not actually have to touch the media.

Large material sheets

These can be used with dry play media, so that the child or children touch the media through the cloth or material and can experience the media without actually becoming messy.

In a group setting some dry cereals, pasta or shredded paper can be placed on a table and a large piece of material can be placed on top. The children can explore the media through the material without actually having to touch the media directly. This experience might also encourage some inquisitiveness and children might want to lift the material to see what is underneath. This may then lead on to some tentative exploration.

Large plastic sheets or foil blankets

Once the children have become used to using the large material sheets you could move on to the use of a large plastic sheet. This can be used with wet or dry media.

Clear plastic is the best to use because then the media can be seen as well as felt, adding to the sensory experience. The children would be able to see the media moving around under the sheet. There may also be some sound as the medium moves under the sheet, which could offer an auditory experience.

Again, the sheet may encourage some more inquisitive children to lift the sheet and further explore the medium, although this might not be such a good idea if you were using wet media.

Plastic zippy bags and laminate pockets

Amounts of a particular medium can be can be placed in seal-fresh zippy bags or laminate pockets, so that it can be pushed around inside the sealed container. This can be useful for one child on her own or many children in a group setting.

The seal-fresh bags are best for use with dry ingredients. The ingredients can be placed in the bag and the bag sealed almost to the end. Then, using a straw, the air can be drawn from the bag by sucking the air out. This will prevent the bag from popping and the contents exploding outwards if the bag is patted too vigorously. Or the air could be left in the bag to enable the contents to move around freely.

Because the bag is clear, the child can see the contents. The bag can be poked, prodded or patted without the child having to come into direct contact with the medium. As it is dry, when it is patted there will also be a satisfying crunching sound as the contents are squashed or moved around inside the bag. The child can also see the contents changing as they are squashed. The sounds and the sights all add to the sensory experiences.

Laminate pockets are best if you want to work with the wetter ingredients. They come in all sizes, but I have found that the A4 or bigger sizes are more useful. If you use smaller sizes than this the pockets do not hold so much and can unseal more readily.

Laminate pockets come with one end sealed. In order to use them effectively you need to seal two more edges using a cool iron, not using the steam setting, and sealing about one centimetre along each edge. Having done this the pocket can be opened along its last unsealed edge and the wet ingredient can be placed inside. This is the difficult bit because the fourth side of the pocket needs to be sealed after the wet medium has been put inside. In order to do this without some of the contents coming out, the bag needs to be folded over enough to allow the contents to stay in the bag while the unsealed edge remains uppermost so that it can be sealed with the iron. It is especially important that each corner is firmly sealed, again using an iron, because the corners are the weakest points of the bag.

The sealed bag can then be placed in front of the child and will allow the child to see the contents and to watch it all moving around inside the bag. He can also pat, poke, prod and slap the bag.

Any ingredient can be placed in these bags, but if it is a *food substance* you must make sure that the pockets are replaced regularly as the contents can perish, which would introduce a health risk. I advise food pockets being used once only.

Some good ingredients to use are:

- baked beans
- ready-made custard
- rice pudding
- Angel Delight
- condensed milk
- paint and cooked spaghetti
- jelly.

These substances are all good to use because they can move around easily in the plastic pockets and there is little or no friction. But remember to change them regularly.

For non-food media it is probably best to use water, paint or other creative substances. These pockets can be kept for longer because the contents do not deteriorate in the same way as food substances do. So a non-messy bag library could be built up with bags ready to be used when needed. Here are some ideas for these:

- coloured water
- water and washing-up liquid

- paint with added washing-up liquid to aid a smoother movement

- water and glitter

- paint, glitter and washing-up liquid.

Some ideas for using paint:

- *A two-coloured variation* can be offered by carefully creating separate sections within the same laminate pocket and filling each with a different coloured substance. You can do this by sealing the pocket down the middle before putting separate media in each half, then sealing the open edges as before.

- *A colour mixing variation* can also be offered. Seal the pocket down the middle, but leave a space at the top of the middle seal. Then place two different colours of paint one in each side of the pocket and seal the fourth side. Initially the paint will remain in its two halves but the more the child pushes or prods the two sections, the paint will move from one side of the pocket to the other and begin to mix, giving some amazingly colourful possibilities.

- *Encouraging tracking.* If the iron is used carefully on its edge it can make seals across the pocket, which can separate the pocket into smaller, thinner pockets. These can be opened carefully at the top by blowing and paint poured down into them. If pouring proves too difficult, you can blow the paint in with a straw! Once this is done, the pocket can then be sealed at the top in the same way as before. In this variation, the pocket can be used to encourage tracking from one side to another as the child follows the paint with his eyes as he pushes or prods it along through the mini-pockets within the plastic.

Some more ideas for ingredients that could be used in the pockets are:

- crayon shavings and water
- grass cuttings and water
- coloured sand and water
- coloured rice
- coloured pasta
- flour and glitter
- confetti shredded paper of different colours
- coloured feathers
- dry tapioca (the uncooked balls move around like the polystyrene balls in a bean bag)
- dried pulses
- foil confetti in all sorts of shapes and colours available in craft shops.

You should remember that the seals on the pockets will eventually break down, so these must be checked regularly to avoid messy surprises. Also paint can dry out even in the plastic bags, and so these also have to be checked prior to use to make sure they are still functional.

These activities will help to encourage even the most reticent or tactile defensive child to experience messy play in a safe manner and will build confidence and experience that will help the child to move on and try new (and perhaps more messy!) experiences later on.

12 PRE-WRITING SKILLS

Yes, unbelievably, messy play can be used to encourage pre-writing skills. All children like to make marks on paper and then like to give it meaning. I used to work in a pre-school, where one of the daily activities was mark making. It was encouraged at all points of the day. If there was a shop in the role-play corner, then paper and pencils were always left to encourage emergent writing (e.g. shopping lists) or if there was a post office theme, we would get them to write letters to friends.

Whenever the children created a picture or a model to take home they were asked to make marks and 'write their names' on the picture.

Of course, structured writing skills were also fostered through activities such as writing over letters and names. There was always a writing table set out where the children could come to follow activities such as tracing, stencils or cutting and sticking, but there was also lots of paper for free drawing.

When the children drew a picture they always wanted to talk about it and wanted me to write down what they said. As they got older they wanted to make their own writing on the paper. We also encouraged mark making in the sand tray when dry sand was used.

When I came to work in the Portage service I wanted to bring these experiences with me and incorporate them and possibly extend them in a messy play session. With a lot of the children we work with it is difficult to find pens and pencils that can be manipulated to make marks. In our service we usually use the triangular shaped chunky pens and pencils that encourage a good grip. However, when the use of pens is too challenging for the child, messy play can be used to build hand grasping and fine motor skills until pens can be used appropriately.

Messy play can be effective in encouraging this development because you do not need any specialist equipment, you use what you already have in your home or group. You do not need to use reams and reams of paper, and in our environmentally conscious age that has to be an advantage.

When children are given a sheet of paper they tend to make marks in one corner and then either want a clean sheet of paper or to turn the paper over and use the other side. It would appear that once a mark has been made, however big or small, a clean sheet is necessary. I am sure that we all know the wonder of a clean sheet of paper that no one else has used. It is crisp, clean and smooth and almost seems to be inviting you to make the first mark. However, once those first few words are written it loses its novelty and its cleanness. As an adult you know you have to go on and fill the whole sheet, and there is a joy and a satisfaction in doing that.

Children do not see this, they see a mess and they want to start again. Using messy play in the pre-writing stage of development, there is no paper and no wastage. You just clear the surface and start again.

EQUIPMENT

Ideally what is needed is a clear, clean smooth surface on which the medium can be moved around. A black surface is good to use for a light-coloured medium because the contrast between the lightness of the medium and the darkness of the surface makes the marks stand out. Similarly, a clear or a white surface is useful for the darker medium. To create these effects you could use:

- stiff black card
- a small blackboard
- a large mirror
- a piece of white polythene
- a piece of black polythene
- a piece of foil survival blanket
- a whiteboard.

To encourage circular movements, use circular objects or pieces of material and get the child to follow the circular shape in his mark making. For this you could use:

- a large white plastic plate, such as those used at a barbecue
- a ready-made pizza tray
- a circular mirror
- a large frying pan
- a large non-stick saucepan
- an enamelled saucepan.

For drawing straight lines, use items that will encourage the child to follow the line from left to right across the table. For example:

- a plain long thin sandwich tray
- a rectangular plastic tray (from a ready-made meal or ice-cream dessert)
- a ruler (which has an indentation in the middle and can be followed with the finger)
- a thin rectangular piece of black or white plastic.

When the child is ready to move on to making cross marks then a template can be made of card or plastic which can be placed in the medium on the tray and the child can move her finger along following the lines. When the template is lifted up the child can then see the impression she has made in the medium.

Media

To encourage pre-writing skills, you need to use a medium that flows easily and can be smoothed over to create a clean surface to work on. If you are using a wet medium then it needs to be fairly thick so that the mixture does not immediately revert to its smooth state once a mark is made in it.

Dry media options would be:

- flour
- lentils
- sand
- coloured rice
- glitter
- milkshake powder
- compost
- tea leaves
- fine sawdust
- rice krispies.

Wet media choices are:

- cornflour mixed with water
- condensed milk
- shaving foam
- aerosol cream
- mashed potato (not thick)
- golden syrup
- milkshake powder mixed thickly with water
- Angel Delight
- custard powder mixed with water
- ready-made custard
- instant chocolate mixed thickly with water.

With all of this equipment and media to choose from you have a great variety of experiences with which to foster children's pre-writing skills before they move on to using pens and paper. The children have freedom to experiment over and over again, and because the surfaces can be cleared quickly, they can repeatedly be made ready for the child to start again.

In addition to this, the use of different materials offers the possibility of a lovely sensory experience. There are sights, smells and sounds and, if the child wishes, tastes to encounter.

USING EQUIPMENT TO MAKE MARKS

The child will generally be using his own hands and fingers to make marks, however, as an alternative and when the opportunity is appropriate, it is possible to use equipment.

Before moving from using fingers to make marks to using pens which have to be manipulated properly, you can try various implements that will successfully make marks without the need to hold them in a particular way. You could use anything available that is safe and that would produce a mark in any of the media. For example:

- straws
- wooden spoons
- lolly sticks (wooden and plastic)
- plastic spoons
- short pieces of dowel
- an old clean toothbrush.

To make marks in a controlled way using paint, you could collect empty deodorant bottles with roller balls on the end. Wash them thoroughly and make sure they are clean and dry. Remove the roller ball and fill the tube with paint. Replace the roller ball and then use it to make marks with the paint. This is a controlled way of using paint for those children who do not yet have the fine motor skills to hold and use a paint brush. It produces no large blobs or sudden drops of paint, just nice smooth marks.

Having become familiar with the use of these implements, the child's next step will be to move on to pens, pencils, crayons and chalks, initially the chunky sort, which can be held in a whole hand grasp, and then, as hand control improves, the smaller ones that can be held in a controlled tripod grasp.

The pace at which the child may be able to move through these stages will vary and you will need to be patient. However, the development of all stages can be assisted by engaging in appropriate messy play activities.

13 THINGS TO REMEMBER

Messy Play is Messy

I feel like I am repeating myself, and perhaps by now you all know, but I will say it again… 'Messy play is messy.' It does not matter whether you are using wet or dry, sticky or free-flowing media… messy play is messy. It is this thought that you have to remember when you embark upon messy play. It does not matter whether you engage in this in a group in a classroom or in a home, with lots of children or just the one, it will still be messy. Therefore you will need to be prepared and forearmed and I will just put down a few reminders to help with this.

Preconceived ideas

As I have stated before people have some very funny ideas about messy play. For some people the whole idea of mess is just unthinkable. Whenever I have broached the possibility of messy play, I have met with one of two responses. Either it is excitement and expectation, or total horror; there does not seem to be any middle ground! Some people are willing to try anything to reach their child, others are concerned how something so obscure as this can possibly be any help at all. Behind all of these there is also the worry about just how messy is messy. Sometimes I think that I should use the term sensory play, as this would be much better received, but I don't think it sounds so exciting at all.

Past experiences

In some situations many new ideas will already have been tried, and there will be expectations that this new idea will also come to nothing, so it will not be fully supported and will not work as well as it might.

Another attitude, especially if you are a new face in a situation, is that so and so would never have done this, and the 'ghost' of the previous professional is ever with you. Once again, without full support from the team, the session is unlikely to be successful. Or you may need to overcome the fact that someone else tried this before and it did not help at all, and so everyone is reluctant to engage again.

Fear of the unknown

I speak for myself as much as for anyone else when I say that I know and understand this reaction. I really hate going into new situations, and I can create such unrealistic expectations that my fear of the whole thing can be totally unreasonable. However, I know from experience that this can be exactly the reaction when one mentions messy play. Thus, fear can lead to resistance and a lack of desire to partake on the part of the adult, which can transfer to the child and can create quite a fearful situation for all concerned.

These are all quite normal responses, and in many respects are to be expected rather than the more exciting 'Let's do it!' which I have to say I do not come across very often. What is to be remembered is that this is a partnership. We are all working together to meet the needs of the child and we need to place the child at the centre of all we do. We do not want to so alienate each other that we cannot work together effectively in order to help the child.

When working with families in a home situation, it is obvious to say but it is *their home* and you are in a privileged position to be there.

You have been invited into that home, you are working there as a guest and you have to be considerate of the wishes of the family.

I have worked with lots of families over the past four years, and although some have been initially reticent, all have eventually become happy to agree to engage with messy play in all its fullness. If you enter the situation with the attitude 'I know best' and 'We are going to do this no matter what,' you will soon hit a brick wall. If you have a positive attitude and start with activities with which the family is comfortable, you will eventually gain their confidence and be able to move on to other activities.

All these things also need to be remembered when working in a classroom where you are a guest worker, and when you are in a group situation. However, in a group situation there is the advantage of group dynamics or, to put it bluntly, peer pressure. If one member of the group is enthusiastic then he or she will soon enthuse the rest of the group and the worries will soon disappear. This regularly happens with groups of children. There only needs to be one child who ventures to put his hand into the big bowl of gloop, and the others soon follow him.

BE PREPARED...

...to be flexible

You may go along to the home or the group prepared and planning to do X, Y and Z. However, once there you may find that the child just does not want to engage in what you have brought along. Or it may be that even with your sheet and overalls, the family thinks what you are bringing is just too messy and they do not wish to engage.

When this happens, you have to be prepared to change the activity, and it is always helpful to have one or two ideas up your sleeve just in case a sudden change is called for. In a group situation it might be that someone in the group has a specific sensitivity to the activity that you have brought along. In case this happens, have another medium ready at hand that will achieve the same ends, but which will enable the sensitive child to be able to take part easily. By being flexible and able to change direction in this way, nobody will need to feel uncomfortable or that they are causing a problem, and everything should be able to carry on smoothly with the minimum of disruption.

...to think again

However well prepared you are, however many alternatives you have considered or made plans for, you may just find that the session is not successful. The child may not wish to take part, or the group will engage once and then find something else to do, or the adults accompanying are very negative and actively discourage the children from taking part. It may be that something happened before the visit that set the tone for the whole session and meant that all you had planned would no longer work well.

When this happens it is all too easy to become disillusioned and to go away dissecting every little second of the activity and coming to the conclusion that you made a bad choice and that that activity should never have happened. It is easy to blame yourself and believe that little voice which suddenly appears in your head and tells you that you don't know what you are doing, that everyone thinks you are mad, that they were all laughing at you... and that it was all your fault!

When that happens you have to decide that tomorrow is another day and that you can always try again. No experience is ever wasted and just because it did not turn out as you wished does not mean the children did not learn anything.

AND REMEMBER...

...the dentist

There is a concern that messy play involves too many sweet media. In today's atmosphere of healthy eating, it is appropriate to be concerned about the substances used in messy play. Most of the substances are used for tactile experiences and gross motor experiences rather than any deliberate eating. Whilst I do use some for gustatory experiences it is only very occasionally.

When messy play is used for taste, then it should be used immediately after a meal when the salivary glands are already active and should not be used a long time before a meal or a long time after a meal. It would seem that even a small piece of a sweet substance can cause great damage to a child's teeth, so you must be very careful when using sweet, or acidic food substances during messy play. Cleaning teeth straight afterwards is also not advisable because this can encourage over-stimulation of the salivary glands, which can also cause problems in the teeth.

Therefore, if food is to be tasted more frequently, use food which is more bland but which has a good tactile sensation. Some examples:

- porridge oats
- cottage cheese
- natural yoghurt
- grated cheese
- dried pasta
- plain cooked pasta
- cooked pulses
- cooked cauliflower (less acidic than tomatoes and good for squeezing)
- mashed potatoes
- Weetabix (wet and mixed with water)
- rice puddings made with milk but no sugar
- cooked cous-cous
- cooked bulghur wheat
- gelatine with no flavouring or colourings
- cornflour and water
- custard powder and water, but no sugar

- coloured water
- mashed bananas
- cooked apples but no sugar
- crushed crackers
- all kinds of flours
- mushy peas
- cooked rice
- flaked rice
- small cherry tomatoes
- semolina
- tapioca (cooked with water)
- uncooked pastry
- bread dough
- breadcrumbs fresh and toasted
- popcorn (cooked and uncooked)
- grated carrots or any grated vegetables.

I understand why dentists are concerned, but I am convinced that always restricting the children to bland food will mean that they will miss out on some wonderful gustatory and olfactory experiences. Therefore, remember to use some sweet substances to arouse taste and smell, but ensure that they are used sparingly. A dentist has told me that when a child eats a sweet substance, it does not matter how large an amount he eats, the acid attack will occur for 20 minutes after the child finishes eating. The dentist's advice to overcome this problem is to give a small piece of cheese to eat because this will neutralize the acids in the child's mouth.

...strong flavours

Highly flavoured materials should be used with caution. Remember my example of the little boy's reaction to banana milkshake, which was totally unexpected by me or his parents (chapter 4).

I have since discovered why this reaction occurred. I attended a workshop run by scientists who specialize in the sense of smell. They said that they have discovered that there is a chemical smell in bananas that some people react quite strongly to. It is that chemical which causes some people to be repulsed by the smell of banana even to the extent of not even being able to be in a room with a banana. It was this chemical that caused the child to react so violently to the banana milkshake. Although this is not a common reaction it is something to be aware of.

. . . AND FINALLY

I hope that with all these 'things to remember' I have not deterred you from trying some messy play. These are all just cautionary notes and are likely to relate to only a few very rare occurrences. I hope instead that all my varying examples will have caused you to smile and maybe to laugh, but above all I hope that they will inspire you to go ahead and have a go. Messy play is meant to be enjoyed by all involved. I hope that this little book will have given you ideas that you want to try and that you use them with the expectation that something good will happen. So go ahead, try it and have fun!

But remember that this is only the beginning. I am only giving you ideas to start your adventure. As you delve deeper you will adjust and change things to suit your and the children's needs, and the journey that you have begun will flow smoothly with not too many dead ends and will come to a satisfying conclusion.

Further Reading

Beard, R.M (1974) *An Outline of Piaget's Developmental Psychology.* London: Routledge and Kegan Paul.

Featherstone, S. (2002) *The Little Book of Messy Play.* Lutterworth: Featherstone Education.

Featherstone, S. (2006) *Messy Play: Progression in Play for Babies and Children.* Lutterworth: Featherstone Education.

Gee, R. and Meredith, S. (1993) *Entertaining and Educating your Preschool Child.* London: Usborne.

Lear, R. (1977) *Play Helps: Toys and Activities for Handicapped Children.* London: Heineman Health.

Lear, R. (1998) *Look at it this Way: Toys and Activities for Children with a Visual Impairment.* Oxford: Butterworth and Heinemann.

Longhorn, F. (1988) *A Sensory Curriculum for Very Special People.* London: Souvenir Press.

National Portage Association (1998) *Portage Curriculum for Professional Development: Working with Children with Profound and Multiple Learning Difficulties.* Yeovil: National Portage Association.

Newman, S. (2008) *Small Steps Forward: Using Games and Activities to Help Your Pre-school Child with Special Needs* (2nd edition). London: Jessica Kingsley Publishers.

Nilsson, L. (1990) *A Child Is Born.* London: Transworld.

Reitzes, F. and Teitelman, B. (1995) *Wonderplay: Interactive and Developmental Games, Crafts and Creative Activities for Infants, Toddlers and Preschoolers.* Philadelphia, PA: Running Press.

Schwartz, S. (2004) *The New Language of Toys: Teaching Communication Skills to Children with Special Needs.* Bethesda, MD: Woodbine House.

Sonksen, P. and Stiff, B. (1991) *Show Me What My Friends Can See.* London: Institute of Child Health.

Ware, J., Jones, W., Martin, P., Alton, L. and Loftus, P. (2006) *Routes for Learning: Assessment Materials for Learners with Profound Learning Difficulties and Additional Disabilities.* Cardiff: Qualifications and Curriculum Group.

Index